GW01072081

LES EDITIONS DU MONT-TONNERRE
Founder and Publisher: Wilfried LeCarpentier
Editor-at-Large: William Landmark
Managing Editor: Caroline Favreau

AUTHENTIK CHIC PARIS
Fashion and Shopping Consultant: D'Arcy Flueck
Restaurants, Wine and Food Consultant: Gérard Poirot
Project Editor: Nicola Mitchell
Copy Editors: Jessica Fortescue, Natasha Edwards
and Sandra Iskander
Researcher: Jessica Phelan
Editorial Assistant: Jennifer Parker

Creative Director: Lorenzo Locarno
Artistic Director: Nicolas Mamet
Graphic Designer: Amélie Dommange
Layout Artist: Marie-Thérèse Gomez
Cover Design and Packaging: Nicolas Mamet
Cartographer: Map Resources
Map Illustrator: Kouakou
Pre-Press and Production: Studio Graph'M, Paris

GLOBE PEQUOT PRESS
President and Publisher: Scott Watrous
Editorial Director: Karen Cure

ACKNOWLEDGEMENTS
Special thanks to Marie-Christine Levet, Scott Watrous, Karen Cure,
Gunnar Stenmar, Gérard Paulin, Pierre Jovanovic, Jacques Derey,
Bruno de sa Moreira, Steven Cass and Francesco Betti

Uncover the Exceptional

The Authentik book collection was born out of a desire to explore beauty and craftsmanship in every domain and in whatever price bracket. The books describe the aesthetic essence of a city, homing in on modern-day artisans who strive for perfection and whose approach to their work is as much spiritual as commercial. Written by specialist authors, the guides delve deep into the heart of a capital and, as a result, are excellent companions for both locals and nomadic lovers of fine living. Their neat size, made to fit into a suit or back pocket, make them easy and discreet to consult, and their elegant design and insider selection of addresses will ensure that you get to the heart of the local scene and blend in perfectly with it. There is even a notebook at the back for some cerebral scribbling of your own. In all, Authentik Books are the perfect accessory for uncovering the exceptional, whether in the arts, fashion, design or gastronomy.

Wilfried LeCarpentier
Founder and Publisher

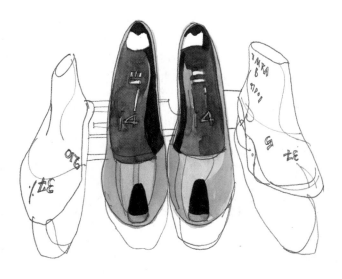

Rodolphe Menudier
25 avenue Montaigne, 8th

Contents

How to Use This Guide

Ever felt like jumping in a taxi at Roissy airport and saying, "Take me to the centre of things!?" Well, this book does the work of a very knowledgeable taxi driver.

Chic Paris consists of ten chapters of insider information on the places that give the French capital and its inhabitants its inimitable elegance. As well as fashion boutiques, accessories stores and talented craftsmen, the guide leads you to the personal shoppers and beauty specialists who can help you acquire that *je ne sais quoi* of French style. There's information on the most chic hotels to stay in, the galleries to frequent, the restaurants to be seen in, and the districts to live should you decide to stay.

The directory at the end of each chapter gives the addresses of the places mentioned, plus the details of other essential stops too numerous to include in the chapter. Use the map references added to the addresses in the directory to find the general location of our listings on the maps at the back of the guide, which cover all the principal streets of central Paris.

Using the **2D BAR CODE** below you can load all the addresses onto a mobile phone with Internet access. This unique aspect of the book enables you to travel extra light.

scan here

How to access content on your mobile phone

If your mobile phone has Internet access and a built-in camera go to

www.scanlife.com

Download the free software that allows your mobile phone to identify the bar code. Downloading takes less than one minute. Then go to your personal file icon, which will appear on your phone's menu screen, and select the icon **Scanlife**. Next, point your camera at the 2D bar code. A sound confirms that the bar code has been recognized. You can then access the directories on your phone.

THE CITY OF
ELEGANT DELIGHTS

Le Bon Marché
24 rue de Sèvres, 7th

Previous page: Palais Royal, with Daniel
Buren's Columns, 1st

01

Many cities claim to possess chic, but only Paris invented it. The word first appeared in the late 1850s, a boom time for Paris with the flowering of the Second Empire under Napoléon III. *Chic* originally meant "subtlety" but this was hardly what was going on at the time. The imperial court, with the Empress Eugénie as style icon, made the French capital the scintillating lode star in the fashion galaxy, and demand for luxury goods rocketed as the bourgeoisie flocked to deck themselves in silks and satins, jewels and furs. Ostentation was the name of the game, to be shown off on the fashionable new boulevards and at the theatre and opera.

The birth of luxury shopping

Charles Frederick Worth opened the first couture house in 1858, fitting out his aristocratic clients, while **Le Bon Marché** made luxury available to all who could afford it, a temple of commerce decried by one male commentator (perhaps fearful for his wallet) as a "trap for bird-brained women." But the origins of Paris as the world capital of chic go back long before the word itself was born. Renaissance monarch François 1er started the ball rolling by importing artists and artisans from Italy to embellish his court. A century later French luxury reached its zenith with Louis XIV, the Sun King. Versailles was not just a palatial residence for the King, but a showpiece for the French *art de vivre*, where foreign dignitaries would be wowed by furniture, glassware, porcelain, textiles and lace from names that are still the benchmark of quality today – and encouraged to place orders.

When the current head of Cartier, Bernard Fornas, was interviewed on what figure from history he would most have liked to be, he said Louis XIV at Versailles: "You haven't a place in the world with an accumulation of the art of living and of luxury to compare; it was the art of living in refinement."

Exclusive fashion

In the early years of Napoleon's reign, the high-waisted Empire dress was created to draw subliminal parallels with the Roman Empire. It became the rage all over Europe, and aristocrats came to Paris to visit their seamstresses and tailors, and commission exquisite jewels and scents based on those worn by Empress Josephine. The Emperor enforced the exclusivity of French fashion by banning imports of English textiles, promoting French fabric and lace and forbidding ladies to wear the same dress to court more than once.

While seamstresses slaved to complete their gowns, the visitors promenaded on the fashionable rue Saint-Honoré and ate at restaurants such as **Le Grand Véfour** in the Palais Royal. Visiting Paris twice a year to buy your entire wardrobe was still de rigueur for society women into the 1950s – and indeed some fabulously wealthy clients keep up the tradition, renting apartments in the **Hôtel Bristol**, where private fashion shows by the couture houses are arranged for their eyes only.

01

If the centuries of savoir-faire in the realms of fashion, perfumery, jewellery and the decorative arts are one reason for Paris' chic supremacy, there is another factor in the equation: Parisians' own innate sense of style. Fashion writer Lynn Schnurnberger calls it "the mystical scarf-tying gene," but Parisians themselves might call it simply a *je ne sais quoi*. Is it really so effortless?

Behind the scenes those casually elegant creatures you see in Saint-Germain-des-Prés or on rue du Faubourg Saint-Honoré keep up a highly ordered schedule of visits to the hair stylist, manicurist, beautician, dietician, dermotologist, venologist, gynaecologist... and pyschiatrist. This means that Paris has some of the most advanced beauty treatments in the world, and perhaps more hairdressers per square kilometer than anywhere else. The trend has moved from scientific

Le Restaurant du Palais Royal,
110 galerie de Valois, 1st

01

and clinical beauty institutes to the New York-style day spa – a place to relax and be pampered, before rushing on to the next appointment.

"I will tell you about a great place," whispers one well-groomed client to another. These secrets change hands among the chic elite. It might be a skin specialist, a *rémailleur* (invisible mender), a florist or a friend who buys vintage couture. Personal recommendation is paramount, and personal service essential. While the traditional Parisian concierge – a gossip in slippers who watches who goes in and out of your apartment – is a dying breed, a new type of concierge service is on the up: the personal assistant and miracle worker able to arrange anything, from tickets for the opera to flowers when you arrive back from holiday.

Innate style

In France, style and being well-turned out, for both men and women, seems to begin at birth. Paris is a very visual city – not surprising perhaps as it is so very beautiful. Superficial though it is, you will notice the difference in the way people treat you according to how groomed you look. Chic has less to do with labels than with being soigné(e), well-looked after. The French have a highly tuned aesthetic sense and they like to be surrounded by and associated with

Avenue Montaigne, 8th

beauty. This extends to other sensory realms, such as food and wine. Luxury in Paris doesn't mean a show of wealth, but being able to afford the pinnacle of perfection in any art.

01

That is not to say that celebrity does not play a big part. Client lists at chic spas, boutiques or restaurants run like a red carpet check at Cannes, and Paris's legend is largely built on cinematic images. Audrey Hepburn becomes the epitome of Parisian chic in ugly duckling story *Sabrina*; Catherine Deneuve was chosen as the model for Marianne (the symbol of the Republic); Monica Belucci and Vincent Cassel are the reigning king and queen of the **Armani Caffé**, Saint-Germain's most chic watering hole. From Coco Chanel via Inès de la Fressange to Vanessa Paradis, where would chic be without its Parisienne ambassadors? What do they have that makes them so Parisian? These women can dress up or down and still look beautiful. They don't run amok but are *plutôt* discreet. They enjoy simplicity as well as luxury. And they have that uniquely French quality, insouciance. A bit like Paris itself.

HOT SHOPPING AND SARTORIAL DELIGHTS

Galerie du Palais Royal, 1st

Previous page: Chanel
29-31 rue Cambon, 1st

Personal service coupled with the pure aesthetic joy of shopping in Paris make the acquisitive process one of the city's main pleasures. Acquaint yourself with the different shopping neighbourhoods before setting out to make sure you find the one that suits your own style, be it designer label luxe or a more offbeat *bourgeois-bohème* ('bobo') look.

Place Vendôme and rue Saint Honoré

Where better to start your luxury shopping spree than the stamping ground of Coco Chanel in the heart of the Right Bank? On rue Cambon, below the apartments where Mademoiselle entertained her friends, is the **Chanel** boutique, where in 2008 Karl Lagerfeld will celebrate his 25th year with the house.

Far from the classicism and restraint of this ultimate Parisian brand, rue Cambon also supports the fiery Latin inspirations of Venezuelan designer **Oscar Carvallo**, creating the perfect sizzling attire for queens of the night, while cutting edge design is hand-picked by another Venezuelan, **Maria Luisa**, whose ever growing empire of boutiques for both men and women are adored by the fashion cognoscenti.

Just behind, on rue Duphot, **minaPoe** is where you'll find former actress Mina d'Ornano's luxurious cashmeres and knits, many delicately embroidered by hand. Meanwhile, **Amin Kader** transports you to an Italian palazzo with the frescoes in his rue de la Paix boutique, which stocks a wonderful mix of exquisite pashminas and cashmere.

Place Vendôme is the *haute joaillerie* epicentre of Paris, with a sparkling roster that includes Bulgari, Cartier, Chaumet and Van Cleef & Arpels. Most exclusive of the lot is **JAR**, alias Joël Arthur Rosenthal, whose shop is by appointment only, and has a slavish following for his extravagant and exorbitant treasures. Nearby, vintage jewellery fanatics will be in heaven at **Lydia Courteille** and at family-run *bijouterie* **Dary's**.

The latter is on rue Saint-Honoré, one of Paris's premier fashion streets since before the French Revolution. Here you'll also find **John Galliano**, and lingerie doyennes **Chantal Thomass** and **Fifi Chachnil**. Thomass's heavenly boudoir boutique is the place to find the exquisitely crafted corsets adored by burlesque artiste Dita Von Teese. The burlesque revival is also right on time for Fifi Chachnil's ultra-feminine lingerie, which will make you feel like a 1950s pin-up. At number 213 is style temple **Colette**, the original concept store with its ever-changing selection of hip fashion and designer gadgets, which generates tourism for Paris all on its own. The Marché Saint-Honoré is worth a detour, too, especially for **45 rpm**'s mix of Japanese streetwear and accessories.

The arcades of Palais Royal, built as a pleasure garden by the roguish Duc d'Orléans and a major seedbed of the French Revolution, is now a calm oasis of shop-filled cloisters. **Pierre Hardy**, who designs the footwear for Hermès, sells his own creations in a sleek boutique here. The Palais's most long-standing fashion resident is **Didier Ludot**, who has populated several boutiques with his stunning vintage couture collections, including one devoted entirely to **La Petite Robe Noire**.

Back on rue Saint-Honoré is **Astier de Villatte**, whose white-glazed earthenware has a chic château-lifestyle appeal. To the north, on rue Chabanais, **The Different Company** is the place to find the perfect perfume gift, restrained and beautiful fragrances created by perfumer Jean-Claude Ellena, while **Jean-Paul Gaultier** keeps up his *enfant terrible* stance on rue Vivienne.

East of Place des Victoires, rue Etienne Marcel has a host of urban outfitters, such as the cutting-edge **Kabuki Homme & Femme**. **Christian Louboutin**'s sassy red soles are sold on rue Jean-Jacques Rousseau,

02

Amin Kader
1 rue de la Paix, 2nd

and the master works in the same building. Don't be fazed by l'**Eclaireur** on rue Hérold. You must buzz to enter this secret apartment, but once inside you will be more than impressed by the artful mix of designer clothing and decorative items.

02

Faubourg Saint-Honoré and the Golden Triangle

With a concentration of fashion's big names unrivalled anywhere in the world, rue du Faubourg Saint-Honoré and the "Golden Triangle" – the name given to the triangle formed by the Champs Elysées, avenue George V and avenue Montaigne – is Paris's prime shopping district for those craving the ultimate in luxury.

Before launching into your fashion foray, stock up on presents to take home. Just off place de la Madeleine children will be delighted with a *cadeau* from the classic children's toy store **Le Nain Bleu**, a favourite with the well-mannered and supremely groomed tiny Parisian set. The branch of **Résonances**, better known for old-fashioned household items, is devoted to well-being and beauty – unusual bathroom items include ecological bamboo fibre towels. Among Madeleine's many luxury food shops, **Maison de la Truffe** sets itself apart for its excellent range of both truffles, real and chocolate, as well as foie gras and other gastronomic goodies. Then detour down rue Royale, for the ultimate French tablewares from porcelain house **Bernardaud**, glassmaker **Lalique** and silversmith **Christofle**. All work with contemporary designers as well as producing their historic lines.

Descending rue du Faubourg Saint-Honoré, the west-ward continuation of rue Saint-Honoré, hot becomes progressively more *haute*. In order from Madeleine, **Lanvin** sells its sexy and sophisticated clothes and bags in two gorgeously decorated houses at numbers 15 (menswear) and 22 (womenswear). Just further along is **Hermès**, which has expanded from saddles and silk scarves to an entire universe of understated classic chic. Hot for tripping the light fantastic since Bruno Frisoni took over, **Roger Vivier** is a great revival story. The inventor of the stiletto once again produces fabulous feather-, crystal- and snakeskin-encrusted Cinderella slippers and has reissued Catherine Deneuve's *Belle du Jour* demure but oh-so-sexy square-toed Mary-Janes.

Chloé is at number 54 and **Christian Lacroix** has his extravagant shopfront opposite the Hôtel Bristol. More conservatively, Arthur de Soultrait has created a preppy, polo universe at **Vicomte Arthur**, selling men's shirts, ties and other accessories in a splendid array of colour combinations. **Hartwood**, across the road, is the trusted outfitter for many French politicians.

Rue la Boétie lands you in the middle of the Champs-Elysées part of the Golden Triangle, the area commandeered by **Louis Vuitton** and friends in the 1930s to protect their luxury world from the march of gaudy commerce on the Champs. Vuitton's flagship store, on the corner of avenue George V, is the lynchpin of it all, and its sheer scale and unusual art installations have been wowing visitors since reopening after total refurbishment in 2005. Though **Givenchy** and Yves Saint Laurent haute couture are on avenue George V, and Jean-Paul Gaultier has a store here, it is **Balenciaga** that is the real draw. Artist Dominique Gonzalez-Foerster imagined a setting reminiscent of 2046 with an underground zone with asteroids, coloured lights and a watery passage in which to display Nicolas Ghesquière's retro-futuristic clothes.

Rounding Place de l'Alma you'll soon find yourself on Fashion Avenue, avenue Montaigne. Among the canon of luxury names, **Dior** has a string of shops ranging from women's ready-to-wear designed by John Galliano to Kris van Assche's creations for **Dior Homme** via **Baby Dior** and flamboyant jewellery confected by Victoire de Castellane at **Dior Joaillerie**.

Cutting up rue François 1er, you may be surprised to see **Zadig & Voltaire de Luxe**, the hip casual mini-chain

Hermès
24 rue du Faubourg Saint-Honoré, 8th

making a foray into high-end luxury fashion with its easy-to-wear clothes. Beauty buffs know to head to **La Parfumerie Générale,** just off rue Marbeuf, for its hard-to-find products. Owner Victoire de Taillac, sister of jeweller Marie-Hélène, used to work as a publicist for Colette, and has a great sense of what the next big thing will be where beauty is concerned.

02

The aristocratic 7th

The aristocratic 7th *arrondissement* around rue du Bac is the home to many of Paris's style eccentrics: **Loulou de la Falaise,** a former muse of Yves Saint Laurent, has been charming clients since 2003 with her distinctively French style on rue de Bourgogne. Designed to feel like a visit to a friend's home, this is Paris shopping at its best: relaxed and oh so stylish. Chic Parisian mothers-to-be and French celebrities frequent **1 et 1 font 3** on nearby rue de Solférino and, crossing over boulevard Saint-Germain-des-Prés, you'll find interior designer **India Mahdavi,** the next generation's Christian Liaigre.

This is the area to pick up clothes and accessories for the impeccable 7th look. **Madeleine Gely** has been selling umbrellas on boulevard Saint-Germain since 1834 (definitely not ones to leave behind). On rue Montalembert near the chic Hôtel Montalembert, **Lucien Pellat-Finet,** revered in Japan, has updated the cashmere twinset with an injection of youth and humour, which can be complemented with stunning jewellery by **Anaconda**, made using only white gold and the most feminine pale pink diamonds. Minutes away on rue de Beaune, vintage lovers will adore **Catherine Arigoni** who offers a slice of ladylike history.

Make a detour here to visit Karl Lagerfeld's 7L bookshop, an essential port of call for hard-to-find fashion editions. Almost next door, is **Design Bazar**, a private apartment filled with exceptional French and Scandinavian furniture from the 1950s to 70s, scoured from across Europe by owner Diane de Polignac.

At **Iunx** – fascination in Greek – discover an astounding compilation of unisex scents in a gallery-like environment. Still on the perfume trail, step into the dedicated scent cabins at **Editions de Parfums Frédéric Malle**. Malle has a cleverly edited collection created by nine of his favourite perfumers, including the latest, aptly named, French Lover. His rue de Grenelle boutique comes as a refreshing change in a street almost entirely devoted to shoes – including the **Bruno Frisoni** store. Other such anomalies are **Rare**, an accessory fanatic's dreamland, and the ultra-feminine lingerie of Belgian **Carine Gilson**, which is certain to inspire a few florid daydreams.

The northern end of boulevard Raspail is where you'll find another graduate of the couture set: Balmain and Valentino alumnus **Georgina Brandolini** creates luxury separates and swimwear. For men, **Shipton & Heneage** offers well-made, classic English-style shoes. More surprisingly this is also the area for cutting-edge design and furniture stores, among them **Edifice** and **Cassina**.

02

Rue du Bac is the perfect street for anyone wanting to lavish attention on home and hearth. **Christian Liaigre**, known for his sophisticated modern take on Art Deco style, is at number 42, followed by **La Paresse en Douce**, a tender deco dream come true, while **Le Prince Jardinier** has inspired a new generation to take up spade and hoe with the ultra-chic gardening accessories created by Prince Louis Albert de Broglie. Meanwhile **R & Y Augousti**'s luxurious mix of snakeskin- and leather-covered furniture and fashion accessories has already graced American *Vogue*.

The beloved **Bon Marché**, Paris's earliest department store, occupies a building designed by Gustave Eiffel. Its Grand Epicerie carries imported foodstuffs from around the world, while Balthazar, the men's department, is one-stop shopping at its best. Another mainstay for the Paris dandy, **Arnys** has dressed legends like Picasso, Sartre and Le Corbusier.

Editions de Parfums Frédéric Malle
37 rue de Grenelle, 7th

Saint-Germain-des-Prés

The intellectual heartland of Paris is now home to fabulously chic boutiques and a host of designer labels, but retains an artistic allure with the many galleries along rue de Seine. Shopping here is a joy if you pepper it with stops on Saint-Germain's legendary café terraces to watch the well-dressed world go by. At the bustling carrefour de la Croix Rouge crossroads, pop into **Robert Clergerie** to check out the incredible chunkily sculpted soles and ultra-soft leather shoes. Then walk up rue des Saints-Pères to find sensual lingerie by **Sabbia Rosa** (worn by Madonna, no less), while next door, Canadian-born **Tara Jarmon** encapsulates the feminine spirit of Paris in her flirty dresses. A little further up, **Zef** sells impeccably cut children's clothes that will make you wish you were six again.

Walk down to the Seine, where **Dries van Noten** has installed itself in a former bookshop on the quai Malaquais, before heading down to the heart of Saint-Germain via rue Bonaparte. At number 17, **Mona** is a pristine boutique filled with choice designer wear by the likes of Alexander McQueen, Missoni and Bottega Veneta. Cross-streets rue Jacob and rue de l'Abbaye are where you'll find the perfect baubles to adorn your new outfits: bright semi-precious stones at **Adeline** and daintily crocheted necklaces and brooches at

02

Yesim Chambrey. This Turkish designer also creates sublimely feminine womenswear in unusual natural materials such as bamboo. Check out also the chic furnishing fabrics and home accessories at **Pierre Frey**. Nearby Carrefour de Buci bustles with food and clothes shoppers. Here, **Comptoir des Cotonniers** is always a good stop for its simple but well-made separates.

In the heart of Saint-Germain is the designer most synonymous with the area, **Sonia Rykiel**, who has a string of boutiques ranging from her stylish ready-to-wear to her more affordable Sonia label to a store selling the most chic sex toys around. **Gérard Darel** is another name for classic, yet fashionable separates and also makes soft suede bags. **Yves Saint Laurent** is, of course, *rive gauche* with his men's and women's boutiques on Place Saint-Sulpice, where Christian Lacroix also has a Left Bank presence. On rue Saint-Sulpice you'll find **Catherine Memmi**'s sophisticated loungewear, with housewares and furniture to match. Turn down rue de Tournon for jewellery by **Marie-Hélène de Taillac** and the cashmere-addict's fantasy land of **Le Cachemirien**.

Proximity to the Jardin du Luxembourg means proximity to some of Paris's best childrenswear. Still on rue de Tournon, **Bonpoint** is a must-see; the top-of-the-range children's store is housed in the beautiful 17th-century Hôtel de Brancas, and has its own stylish restaurant. **Antik Batik**'s rue de Vaugirard boutique includes its fairytale dresses for little girls. Following the road round the park to the left brings you to rue Madame and **Oona L'Ourse** – classic yet chic childrenswear for those hoping to impose the groomed French look on their little ones. Children, teenagers, madame and even monsieur all love **A.P.C.**'s simple, casual clothes with Gallic flair.

02

The Marais

Paris's former marshes on the Right Bank attract a flamboyant group of style setters. Azzedine Alaïa and Christian Lacroix are both residents, and the area's winding 17th-century streets are packed with tiny boutiques, as well as cutting-edge art and design galleries. Here you'll find the more hip, quirky, original and vintage stockists – it's the kind of place Vanessa Paradis, Kylie Minogue and Maggie Cheung like to shop. The southern half, in the 4th *arrondissement*, has more established names, with **Issey Miyake** on Place des Vosges, his **Pleats Please** on rue des Rosiers and **A-POC** on rue des Francs Bourgeois, along with the originators of the Parisian jeans-and-sweater look, **Zadig et Voltaire**. Its menswear store is on rue Pavée, along with **Caravane**, which is a must for anyone wanting to cultivate the style

Azzedine Alaïa
7 rue du Moussy, 4th

of glossy interiors magazine *Côté Sud* at home. **Antik Batik** displays its filmy, sequined creations on rue de Turenne, not far from Place des Vosges, and **Azzedine Alaïa**'s own stunning showroom is on rue de Moussy, just off rue de Rivoli. While in this lower part of the Marais pop down to **Papier +**, a cult favourite with New York fashion editors for its notebooks.

02

Rue Vieille du Temple is the street to take for boutique shopping, particularly as you reach the northern stretch, which with rue de Poitou, rue Charlot and the streets around the Carreau du Temple, has been newly christened the *haut* Marais. Start with the cult hand-beaded handbags by **Jamin Puech** at number 68, now with collectable status. The Hepburn-era forms of **Paule Ka** are at 93, followed by **Yukiko**'s boudoir-boutique at 97: this Japanese Parisienne combines her own silky bias-cut pieces with tiny vintage dancing shoes, jewellery and vanity cases in a setting reminiscent of Wong Kar-Wai's *In the Mood for Love*. Then there are the ethnic-inspired designs of **Erotokritos** at 99, followed by **Vanessa Bruno** at 100. Don't miss **Galerie Simone** at 124, showcasing one-off fashion pieces and accessories in an art gallery environment.

Trip across rue de Poitou, with **Shine**'s blend of feminine rock-chic, a superb appointment-only vintage couture collection at **Quidam de Revel**, **Jakenko** for a stylish hand-picked wardrobe for men, and **Hoses** for glamorous footwear, to reach rue Charlot. Here, two places evoke the spirit of 18th-century libertine Paris with its salons and dangerous liaisons: lovers looking for the Cyrano de Bergerac touch should visit the **French Letters** vending machine in the Passage de Retz, where 19 expertly written love letters or *billets-doux* are available for €2 each, while Carla Vizzi at **Le Boudoir et sa philosophie** recreates all sorts of rococo fashions, from snuff boxes and nosegays to miniature portraits of your dog. From here on in, it's fashion discovery time. The celebrated Australian designer **Martin Grant** is at number 10, **Samy Chalon**'s boho-chic knitwear at 24, a well-chosen and very feminine selection of designers at **AB33**, current Parisian darling **Gaspard Yurkievich** at 38, and concept store **Surface to Air** at number 68. Not to be left out, **Isabel Marant** has moved into this most happening fashion enclave, on rue de Saintonge. Get here first, because the crowds are sure to follow.

Pigalle, Abbesses and Canal Saint-Martin

The opening of the Hôtel Amour has confirmed the southern Pigalle area (dubbed SoPi) as definitively hip, but those in the know have long had a few select 9th *arrondissement* addresses in their books. One such is

02

Anouschka. This former model receives private sellers, bringing her their vintage collections, in the morning; and buyers – famous fashion designers and celebrities often among them – in the afternoon. Make an appointment to view this incredible couture collection – you never know which famous face you might pass in the elevator. Also worth hunting through are the retro jeans and quirky accessories at **Woch Dom**. For a dash of glam over a glass of Champagne, book an appointment at **Gentry de Paris**; Californian expat Gentry Lane believes every woman should own at least one item of French silk, and her lingerie is made with the finest. Accessory fanatics already know **Karine Arabian** from her days at Chanel; her very modish shoes and bags are found on rue Papillon.

Further north on the Montmartre hill, the bobo streets of Abbesses (now dubbed NoPi or north Pigalle) offer an individual take on fashion. Young designers work in their atelier-boutiques on rue Houdon, while celebrities like Kirsten Dunst have fallen for the design-meets-fashion edge at **Spree**. Also worth checking out is **Kamille**, for its selection of original, subtle clothes, notably knitwear, and accessories created by a group of independent designers, while **Luc Dognin**, who works among the African fabric shops of the spicy Goutte d'Or east of Montmartre, is a name to watch with his

Galerie Vivienne, 2nd

luxurious line of handbags.

Antoine & Lili, who made kitsch chic, also has a boutique in Abbesses, but its flagship stores shed their pastel reflections further east on the water of the Canal Saint Martin. Next door on the quayside are the far more elegant offerings of **Stella Cadente**, and round the corner on rue Beaurepaire, **Ginger Lyly** has a constantly changing array of funky clothes, jewellery and bags. Also worth looking out for is Canadian fashion designer **David Szeto**, known for his sexy streamlined vision – visit his atelier just east of the Canal to place your personal *commande*.

The west side

A foray to the residential 16th and 17th in western Paris is certainly worth the effort when your quest is rewarded with that special something. L'**Espionne**, hidden inside the uninspiring Palais des Congrès, offers a big bang with its mix of cutting-edge international designers, whose daring wares are a little outré for the neighbourhood's ladies who lunch.

Yves Saint Laurent designer Stefano Pilati has his stationary imprinted at **Talmaris**. Meanwhile, **Boutique 22** has loyal following among discerning cigar lovers, for its wide selection which is displayed alongside vintage humidors.

Place Vendôme, Palais Royal and rue Saint-Honoré

45 rpm
4 r du Marché St-Honoré, 1st
Ⓜ Tuileries
Ⓒ 01 47 03 45 45
45rpmstudio.com
✈ 6/M8

Amin Kader
1 r de la Paix, 2nd
Ⓜ Opéra
Ⓒ 01 42 61 33 25
✈ 6/M7

Antik Batik
4 r Cambon, 1st
Ⓜ Concorde
Ⓒ 01 40 15 01 45
✈ 6/K8

Astier de Villatte
173 r St-Honoré, 1st
Ⓜ Palais Royale
Ⓒ 01 42 60 74 13
astierdevillatte.com
✈ 6/M9

Chanel
29-31 r Cambon, 1st
Ⓜ Madeleine
Ⓒ 01 42 86 28 00
chanel.com
✈ 6/K8

Chantal Thomass
211 r St-Honoré, 1st
Ⓜ Tuileries
Ⓒ 01 42 60 40 56
chantalthomass.fr
✈ 6/M9

Christian Louboutin
19 r Jean-Jacques
Rousseau, 1st
Ⓜ Louvre Rivoli
Ⓒ 01 42 36 05 31
christianlouboutin.fr
✈ 7/O9

Colette
213 r St-Honoré, 1st
Ⓜ Tuileries
Ⓒ 01 55 35 33 90
colette.fr
✈ 6/M9

Costume National
5 r Cambon, 1st
Ⓜ Concorde
Ⓒ 01 40 15 04 13
✈ 6/K8

Dary's
362 r St-Honoré, 1st
Ⓜ Tuileries
Ⓒ 01 42 60 95 23
✈ 6/M9

Didier Ludot
20 & 24 galerie de Montpensier
Jardin du Palais Royal, 1st
Ⓜ Palais Royal
Ⓒ 01 42 96 06 56
didierludot.com
✈ 7/N9

The Different Company
3 r Chabanais, 2nd
Ⓜ Pyramides
Ⓒ 01 42 60 12 74
thedifferentcompany.com
✈ 7/N8

L'Eclaireur
10 r Hérold, 1st
Ⓜ Louvre Rivoli
Ⓒ 01 40 41 09 89
leclaireur.com
✈ 7/O9

Fifi Chachnil
231 r St-Honoré, 1st
Ⓜ Tuileries
Ⓒ 01 42 61 21 83
fifichachnil.com
✈ 6/M9

JAR
(by appointment)
7 pl Vendôme, 1st
Ⓜ Opéra
Ⓒ 01 42 96 33 66
✈ 6/L8

Jean-Paul Gaultier
6 r Vivienne, 2nd
Ⓜ Bourse
Ⓒ 01 42 86 05 05
jpgaultier.com
⊕ 7/O7

John Galliano
386 r St-Honoré, 1st
Ⓜ Concorde
Ⓒ 01 55 35 40 40
johngalliano.com
⊕ 6/L8

**Kabuki Homme
& Femme**
25 r Etienne Marcel, 1st
Ⓜ Etienne Marcel
Ⓒ 01 42 33 55 65
⊕ 7/P9

Lydia Courteille
231 r St-Honoré, 1st
Ⓜ Tuileries
Ⓒ 01 42 61 11 71
⊕ 6/M9

Maria Luisa
4 r Cambon, 1st
Ⓜ Concorde
Ⓒ 01 42 60 95 48
⊕ 6/K8

minaPoe
19 r Duphot, 1st
Ⓜ Madeleine
Ⓒ 01 42 61 06 41
minapoe.com
⊕ 6/K7

Oscar Carvallo
10 r Cambon, 1st
Ⓜ Concorde
Ⓒ 01 40 20 12 13
oscarcavallo.com
⊕ 6/K8

La Petite Robe Noire
125 galerie de Valois
Jardin du Palais Royal, 1st
Ⓜ Palais Royal
Ⓒ 01 40 15 01 04
didierludot.com
⊕ 7/N8

Pierre Hardy
156 galerie de Valois
Jardin du Palais Royal, 1st
Ⓜ Palais Royal
Ⓒ 01 42 60 59 75
pierrehardy.com
⊕ 7/N8

02

Faubourg Saint-Honoré and the Golden Triangle

Baby Dior
26 av Montaigne, 8th
Ⓜ Alma Marceau
Ⓒ 01 49 52 01 45
⊕ 5/F8

Balenciaga
10 av George V, 8th
Ⓜ Alma Marceau
Ⓒ 01 47 20 21 11
balenciaga.com
⊕ 5/E7

Bernardaud
11 r Royale, 8th
Ⓜ Concorde
Ⓒ 01 47 42 82 66
bernardaud.fr
⊕ 6/K7

Chloé
56 r du Fbg St-Honoré, 8th
Ⓜ Concorde
Ⓒ 01 44 94 33 00
chloe.com
⊕ 6/J7

Christian Lacroix
73 r du Fbg St-Honoré, 8th
Ⓜ Miromesnil
Ⓒ 01 42 68 79 00
christian-lacroix.com
⊕ 6/I6

Christofle
9 r Royale, 8th
Ⓜ Concorde
Ⓒ 01 55 27 99 13
christofle.com
⊕ 6/K7

Faubourg Saint-Honoré and the Golden Triangle (cont)

Dior Homme
30 av Montaigne, 8th
Ⓜ Alma Marceau
Ⓒ 01 40 73 54 44
dior.com
✛ 5/F8

Dior Joaillerie
28 av Montaigne, 8th
Ⓜ Alma Marceau
Ⓒ 01 47 23 52 39
diorjoaillerie.com
✛ 5/F8

Givenchy
3 av George V, 8th
Ⓜ George V
Ⓒ 01 44 31 51 09
givenchy.com
✛ 5/E7

Hartwood
123 r du Fbg St-Honoré, 8th
Ⓜ St Philippe du Roule
Ⓒ 01 43 59 43 29
✛ 5/G5

Hermès
24 r du Fbg St-Honoré, 8th
Ⓜ Concorde
Ⓒ 01 40 17 47 17
hermes.com
✛ 6/J7

Lalique
11 r Royale, 8th
Ⓜ Concorde
Ⓒ 01 53 05 12 81
cristallalique.fr
✛ 6/K7

Lanvin
15 & 22 r du Fbg St-
Honoré, 8th
Ⓜ Concorde
Ⓒ 01 44 71 31 33
lanvin.com
✛ 6/J7

Louis Vuitton
101 av des Champs
Elysées, 8th
Ⓜ George V
Ⓒ 0810 810 010
vuitton.com
✛ 5/F6

Maison de la Truffe
19 pl de la Madeleine, 8th
Ⓜ Madeleine
Ⓒ 01 42 65 53 22
maison-de-la-truffe.fr
✛ 6/K7

Le Nain Bleu
5 bd Malesherbes, 8th
Ⓜ Madeleine
Ⓒ 01 42 65 20 00
✛ 6/J6

La Parfumerie Générale
6 r Robert Estienne, 8th
Ⓜ F D Roosevelt
Ⓒ 01 43 59 10 62
✛ 5/F7

Résonances
3 bd Malesherbes, 8th
Ⓜ Madeleine
Ⓒ 01 44 51 63 70
resonances.fr
✛ 6/J6

Roger Vivier
29 r du Fbg St-Honoré, 8th
Ⓜ Concorde
Ⓒ 01 53 43 00 85
rogervivier.com
✛ 6/J7

Vicomte Arthur
162 r du Fbg St-Honoré, 8th
Ⓜ St Philippe du Roule
Ⓒ 01 42 56 37 42
vicomte-arthur.fr
✛ 6/J7

Zadig & Voltaire de Luxe
20 r François 1er, 8th
Ⓜ Franklin D. Roosevelt
Ⓒ 01 40 70 97 89
zadig-et-voltaire.com
✛ 5-6/G8

The aristocratic 7th

1 et 1 font 3
3 r de Solférino, 7th
Ⓜ Solférino
Ⓒ 01 40 62 92 15
1et1font3.com
⊕ 10/K10

7L
7 r de Lille, 7th
Ⓜ St-Germain-des-Prés
Ⓒ 01 42 92 03 58
⊕ 10/M11

Anaconda
10 r de Verneuil, 7th
Ⓜ St-Germain-des-Prés
Ⓒ 01 42 60 18 29
⊕ 10/L11

Arnys
14 r de Sèvres, 7th
Ⓜ Sèvres Babylone
Ⓒ 01 485 48 76 99
arnys.fr
⊕ 10/L13

Le Bon Marché
24 r de Sèvres, 7th
Ⓜ Sèvres Babylone
Ⓒ 01 44 39 80 00
lebonmarche.fr
⊕ 10/L13

Bruno Frisoni
34 r de Grenelle, 7th
Ⓜ Rue du Bac
Ⓒ 01 42 84 12 30
brunofrisoni.com
⊕ 10/K12

Cassina
236 bd St-Germain, 7th
Ⓜ Rue du Bac
Ⓒ 01 42 84 92 92
cassina.com
⊕ 10/L12

Carine Gilson
18 r du Grenelle, 7th
Ⓜ Sèvres Babylone
Ⓒ 01 43 26 46 71
carinegilson.com
⊕ 10/L13

Catherine Arigoni
14 r de Beaune, 7th
Ⓜ Rue du Bac
Ⓒ 01 42 60 50 99
⊕ 10/L11

Christian Liaigre
42 r du Bac, 7th
Ⓜ Rue du Bac
Ⓒ 01 53 63 33 66
christian-liaigre.fr
⊕ 10/K12

Edifice
27bis bd Raspail, 7th
Ⓜ Sèvres Babylone
Ⓒ 01 45 48 53 60
⊕ 10/K13

02

Design Bazar
(by appointment)
3 r de Lille, 7th
Ⓜ Rue du Bac
Ⓒ 06 14 74 77 05
designbazar.com
⊕ 10/L11

**Editions de Parfums
Frédéric Malle**
37 r de Grenelle, 7th
Ⓜ Rue du Bac
Ⓒ 01 42 22 77 22
editionsdeparfums.com
⊕ 10/L12

Georgina Brandolini
16 bd Raspail, 7th
Ⓜ Rue du Bac
Ⓒ 01 45 44 27 96
georginabrandolini.com
⊕ 10/K13

India Mahdavi
3 r Las Cases, 7th
Ⓜ Solférino
Ⓒ 01 45 55 67 67
indiamahdavi.com
⊕ 10/J11

The aristocratic 7th (cont)

Iunx
50 r de l'Université, 7th
Ⓜ Rue de Bac
☎ 01 45 44 50 14
iunx.fr
✛ 10/L11

Loulou de la Falaise
7 r de Bourgogne, 7th
Ⓜ Assemblée Nationale
☎ 01 45 51 42 22
loulou-de-la-falaise.com
✛ 10/I11

Lucien Pellat-Finet
1 r Montalembert, 7th
Ⓜ Rue du Bac
☎ 01 42 22 22 77
lucienpellat-finet.com
✛ 10/L11

Madeleine Gely
218 bd St-Germain, 7th
Ⓜ Rue de Bac
☎ 01 42 22 63 35
✛ 10/L12

La Paresse en Douce
97 r du Bac, 7th
Ⓜ Rue de Bac
☎ 01 42 22 64 10
✛ 10/K12

Le Prince Jardinier
116 r du Bac, 7th
Ⓜ Rue du Bac
☎ 01 42 84 84 00
princejardinier.fr
✛ 10/K12

R & Y Augousti
103 r du Bac, 7th
Ⓜ Rue de Bac
☎ 01 42 22 22 21
augousti.com
✛ 10/K12

Rare
22 r de Grenelle, 7th
Ⓜ St Sulpice
☎ 01 42 22 64 40
✛ 10/L13

Shipton & Heneage
11 bd Raspail, 7th
Ⓜ Rue du Bac
☎ 01 45 48 57 26
shipton.fr
✛ 10/K13

Saint-Germain-des-Prés

Accessoire Diffusion
6 r du Cherche Midi, 6th
Ⓜ St Sulpice
☎ 01 45 48 36 08
✛ 10/L13

Adeline
54 r Jacob, 6th
Ⓜ St Germain des Prés
☎ 01 47 03 07 18
✛ 10/M12

Antik Batik
38 r Vaugirard, 6th
Ⓜ Odéon
☎ 01 43 25 30 22
✛ 11-15/N14

A.P.C.
4 r de Fleurus, 6th
Ⓜ Rennes
☎ 01 45 48 72 42
apc.fr
✛ 14/M15

Bonpoint
6 r de Tournon, 6th
Ⓜ Odéon
☎ 01 40 51 98 20
bonpoint.com
✛ 11-15/N14

Le Cachemirien
13 r de Tournon, 6th
Ⓜ Odéon
☎ 01 43 29 93 82
✛ 11-15/N14

Catherine Memmi
11 r St-Sulpice, 6th
Ⓜ Mabillon
Ⓒ 01 44 07 02 02
catherinememmi.com
⊕ 11/N13

Comptoir des Cotonniers
30 r de Buci, 6th
Ⓜ Mabillon
Ⓒ 01 43 54 56 73
comptoirdescotonniers.com
⊕ 11/N12

Dries van Noten
7 quai Malaquais, 6th
Ⓜ St-Germain-des-Prés
Ⓒ 01 44 27 00 40
driesvannoten.be
⊕ 10/M11

Gérard Darel
174 bd St Germain, 6th
Ⓜ St-Germain-des-Prés
Ⓒ 01 45 48 54 80
gerarddarel.com
⊕ 10/L12

Marie-Hélène de Taillac
8 r de Tournon, 6th
Ⓜ Odéon
Ⓒ 01 44 27 07 07
mariehelenedetaillac.com
⊕ 11-15/N14

Mona
17 r Bonaparte, 6th
Ⓜ St-Germain-des-Prés
Ⓒ 01 44 07 07 27
⊕ 10/M12

Oona L'Ourse
72 r Madame, 6th
Ⓜ N-D-des-Champs
Ⓒ 01 42 84 11 94
oonalourse.com
⊕ 10-14/M14

Pierre Frey
2 r de Furstenberg, 6th
Ⓜ St-Germain-des-Prés
Ⓒ 01 46 33 73 00
pierrefrey.com
⊕ 10/N12

Robert Clergerie
5 r du Cherche Midi, 6th
Ⓜ St-Sulpice
Ⓒ 01 42 84 06 14
robertclergerie.com
⊕ 10/L13

Sabbia Rosa
73 r des Sts-Pères, 6th
Ⓜ St Germain des Prés
Ⓒ 01 45 48 88 37
⊕ 10/M12

Sonia Rykiel
175 bd St-Germain, 6th
Ⓜ St-Germain-des-Prés
Ⓒ 01 49 54 60 60
soniarykiel.com
⊕ 10/L12

Tara Jarmon
75 r des Sts-Pères, 6th
Ⓜ St Germain des Prés
Ⓒ 01 45 44 36 14
tarajarmon.com
⊕ 10/M12

02

Yesim Chambrey
1 r de l'Abbaye, 6th
Ⓜ St-Germain-des-Prés
Ⓒ 01 44 27 06 30
⊕ 10/M12

Yves Saint-Laurent-Rive Gauche
6 pl St-Sulpice, 6th
Ⓜ St Sulpice
Ⓒ 01 43 29 43 00
ysl.com
⊕ 10/M13

Zef
55 bis r des Sts-Pères, 6th
Ⓜ St Germain des Prés
Ⓒ 01 42 22 02 93
zef.eu
⊕ 10/M12

The Marais

AB33
33 r Charlot, 3rd
Ⓜ Filles du Calvaire
Ⓒ 01 42 71 02 82
⊕ 7-8/T9

Antik Batik
18 r de Turenne, 3rd
Ⓜ Chemin Vert
Ⓒ 01 44 78 02 00
⊕ 11-12/T11

A-POC
47 r des Francs Bourgeois, 4th
Ⓜ St Paul
Ⓒ 01 44 54 07 05
isseymiyake.com
⊕ 11-12/T11

Azzedine Alaïa
7 r du Moussy, 4th
Ⓜ Hôtel de Ville
Ⓒ 01 42 72 19 19
⊕ 11/R11

**Le Boudoir et
sa philosophie**
18 r Charlot, 3rd
Ⓜ Filles du Calvaire
Ⓒ 01 48 04 89 79
⊕ 7-8/T9

Caravane
6 r Pavée, 4th
Ⓜ St Paul
Ⓒ 01 44 61 04 20
caravane.fr
⊕ 11-12/T12

Delphine Pariente
5 r du Pas de Mule, 3rd
Ⓜ Chemin Vert
Ⓒ 01 44 54 95 59
⊕ 12/U12

Erotokritos
99 r Vieille-du-Temple, 3rd
Ⓜ St Sébastien Froissart
Ⓒ 01 42 78 14 04
⊕ 11-12/T10

French Letters
Passage de Retz,
9 r Charlot, 3rd
Ⓜ Filles du Calvaire
Ⓒ 01 48 04 37 99
⊕ 7-8/T9

Galerie Simone
124 r Vieille-du-Temple, 3rd
Ⓜ St Sébastien Froissart
Ⓒ 01 42 74 21 28
⊕ 11-12/T10

Gaspard Yurkievich
38 r Charlot, 3rd
Ⓜ Filles du Calvaire
Ⓒ 01 42 77 55 48
gaspardyurkievich.com
⊕ 7-8/T9

Hoses
41 r de Poitou, 3rd
Ⓜ St Sébastien Froissart
Ⓒ 01 42 78 80 62
hoses-limited.com
⊕ 11-12/T10

Isabel Marant
47 r de Saintonge, 3rd
Ⓜ Filles du Calvaire
Ⓒ 01 42 78 19 24
⊕ 7-8/T9

Issey Miyake
3 pl des Vosges, 4th
Ⓜ Chemin Vert
Ⓒ 01 48 87 01 86
isseymiyake.com
⊕ 12/U12

Jakenko
18 r de Poitou, 3rd
Ⓜ St Sébastien Froissart
Ⓒ 01 42 71 80 38
⊕ 11-12/T10

Jamin Puech
68 r Vieille-du-Temple, 3rd
Ⓜ St Paul
Ⓒ 01 48 87 84 87
jamin-puech.com
⊕ 11/S11

Martin Grant
10 r Charlot, 3rd
Ⓜ Filles du Calvaire
Ⓒ 01 42 71 39 49
martingrantparis.com
⊕ 7-8/T9

Papier +
9 r Pont Louis-Philippe, 4th
Ⓜ Pont Marie
Ⓒ 01 42 77 70 49
papierplus.com
⊕ 11/R12

Paule Ka
93 r Vieille-du-Temple, 3rd
Ⓜ St Sébastien Froissart
Ⓒ 01 40 29 92 30
⊕ 11-12/T10

Pleats Please
3bis r des Rosiers, 4th
Ⓜ St Paul
Ⓒ 01 40 29 99 66
pleatsplease.com
⊕ 11/S11

Quidam de Revel
(by appointment)
24-26 r de Poitou, 3rd
Ⓜ St Sébastien Froissart
Ⓒ 01 42 71 37 07
quidam-de-revel.com
⊕ 11-12/T10

Samy Chalon
24 r Charlot, 3rd
Ⓜ Filles du Calvaire
Ⓒ 01 44 59 39 16
⊕ 7-8/T9

Shine
15 r de Poitou, 3rd
Ⓜ St Sébastien Froissart
Ⓒ 01 48 05 80 10
⊕ 11-12/T10

Surface to Air
69 r Charlot, 3rd
Ⓜ Filles du Calvaire
Ⓒ 01 49 27 04 58
Surface2air.com
⊕ 7-8/T9

02

Vanessa Bruno
100 r Vieille-du-Temple, 3rd
Ⓜ St Sébastien Froissart
Ⓒ 01 42 77 19 41
vanessabruno.com
⊕ 11-12/T10

Yukiko
97 r Vieille-du-Temple, 3rd
Ⓜ St Sébastien Froissart
Ⓒ 01 42 71 13 41
⊕ 11-12/T10

Zadig et Voltaire
42 r des Francs
Bourgeois, 4th
Ⓜ St Paul
Ⓒ 01 44 54 00 60
zadig-et-voltaire.com
⊕ 11-12/T11

The west side

Boutique 22
22 av Victor Hugo, 16th
Ⓜ Charles de Gaulle
– Etoile
Ⓒ 01 45 01 81 41
boutique22.fr
⊕ 5/C6

L'Espionne
Palais des Congrès, 2 pl
de la Porte Maillot, 17th
Ⓜ Porte Maillot
Ⓒ 01 40 68 23 31
⊕ 1/A4

Talmaris
61 av Mozart, 16th
Ⓜ Ranelagh
Ⓒ 01 42 88 20 20
⊕ Off map

Spree
16 rue de La Vieuville, 18th

Pigalle, Abbesses and Canal Saint-Martin

Anouschka
(by appointment)
6 av du Coq, 9th
Ⓜ Havre Caumartin
Ⓒ 01 48 74 37 00
anouschka.fr
⊕ 2-6/L5

Ginger Lyly
33 r Beaurepaire, 10th
Ⓜ République
Ⓒ 01 42 06 07 73
⊕ 7-8/T7

Spree
16 r de La Vieuville, 18th
Ⓜ Abbesses
Ⓒ 01 42 23 41 40
spree.fr
⊕ 3/O2

Antoine & Lili
95 quai de Valmy, 10th
Ⓜ République
Ⓒ 01 40 37 41 55
⊕ 8/U7

Kamille
53 r d'Orsel, 18th
Ⓜ Abbesses
Ⓒ 01 46 06 69 87
⊕ 3/O2

Stella Cadente
93 quai de Valmy, 10th
Ⓜ République
Ⓒ 01 42 09 27 00
⊕ 8/U7

David Szeto
(by appointment)
56bis r de Châteaudun, 9th
Ⓜ Trinité
Ⓒ 01 45 05 39 36
gentrydeparis.com
⊕ 2-6/M5

Karine Arabian
4 r Papillon, 9th
Ⓜ Cadet
Ⓒ 01 45 23 23 24
karinearabian.com
⊕ 3-7/P5

Woch Dom
69 & 72 r Condorcet, 9th
Ⓜ Anvers
Ⓒ 01 53 21 09 72
⊕ 3/O3

Gentry de Paris
(by appointment)
56bis r de Châteaudun, 9th
Ⓜ Trinité
Ⓒ 01 45 05 39 36
gentrydeparis.com
⊕ 2-6/M5

Luc Dognin
4 r des Gardes, 18th
Ⓜ Château Rouge
Ⓒ 01 44 92 32 16
dogninparis.com
⊕ 3/R1

02

See page 9 to scan the directory

03

CUSTOM DRESSING
FROM TOP TO TOE

John Lobb
21 rue Boissy d'Anglas, 8th

Previous page: Guerlain
68 avenue des Champs Elysées, 8th

As Cartier's chairman Bertrand Fornas says, true luxury is uniqueness, and in these days when luxury labels are everywhere (both the real thing and imitations), a bespoke, one-off creation stands out more than ever as a mark of distinction. Thanks to support from their prêt-à-porter lines, couturiers have been able to continue the grand tradition of Parisian haute couture, keeping alive a host of skills passed down from generation to generation, while high society still demands made-to-measure suits, hats and gloves for The Season's unmissable events.

Haute couture

After surviving years of hardship, even defying the Germans during the world war II, it would be a tragedy if haute couture in Paris died. The clients are few, but the creations are more spectacular than ever in the hands of the new breed of designers such as John Galliano and Nicolas Ghesquière, who have breathed new life into Dior and Balenciaga respectively. Controlled by the *Chambre Syndicale de la Haute Couture,* which upholds the strict rules of the profession, haute couture is far more than a dress that fits like a glove. It is a unique combination of design flair and painstaking, exquisite craftsmanship. Like ballerinas schooled in Russia, only France's *petites mains*, as seamstresses known for their fabulous skills are called, have the exacting training required to produce such treasures. Among the smaller houses to continue in their predecessor's famous footsteps are **Dominique Sirop**, **Gérald Watelet**, **Franck Sorbier** and **Maurizio Galante**, catering to a truly elite, and often royal, clientele.

For the intricate beading or embroidery, the couturiers turn to their *fournisseurs*, workshops whose craftspeople can make the difference between a piece of clothing and a work of art. It is a mutually dependent relationship: over the past few years Chanel has bought six of the oldest workshops that no longer have heirs to run them, and Karl Lagerfeld has designed small clothing collections that showcase their handiwork. The ateliers are free to work for any client. Should you so wish, you can create your own fantasy pieces with the help of **Lemarié**, a famous *plumassier*, working only with feathers, or **Anne Hoguet**, the last atelier devoted to fan-making. **Legeron** is celebrated for its delicate handmade flowers; **Maison Michel** is the couturiers' hatmaker, famed for its panamas and straw hats. A revival in *broderie*, detailed and intricate embroidery, has meant a new life for **Lanel** as well as the illustrious **Lesage**, which opened a school on its premises in 1992.

It is not only the members of the *Chambre Syndicale* who can make to measure. Back on the fashion scene after an extended hiatus is **Hervé L. Leroux**, better known as Hervé Leger. Though his bandage dress may be a thing of the past, Leger has said he may bring it back; for the time being, the most beautiful Grecian-esque gowns are made-to-measure on the premises.

Also continuing the tradition of high fashion is **Alejandra di Andia**, a glamorous Chilean with an enviable sense of style. Alejandra will guide you through the design process from the luxury of her couture salon, able to transform your sartorial dreams from mere idea into reality. A typically Parisian secret is Yolaine de Gourcuff at **Y de G**, who has been making *demi-mesure* (semi-customised clothing) for her friends for years. Enter through the elaborate Lalique glass doors and expect a warm welcome from her daughter, Diane, who will guide you through the bi-annual collection, which can be made in any size or material.

E2 Chatenet has seduced stars like Gwyneth Paltrow with the duo's eclectic restyled vintage pieces; and *haute fourrier* **J. Mendel** has been catering to luxury lovers for decades. As for brides-to-be, the Parisian couture tradition is a girl's dream come true. Visit **Mercerie d'Un Soir** and **Delphine Manivet** for the ultimate

Cadolle Couture
255 rue Saint Honoré, 1st

inspiration for your special day. **Fanny Liautaud**, who began as a *petite main* at Givenchy draws a starry clientele for her wedding dresses and elegant evening wear as well as for seductive lingerie.

Lingerie supremos

A spectacular indulgence, and one which will certainly become an addiction, is made-to-measure lingerie. Poupie Cadolle, the sixth generation of women at **Cadolle Couture**, will personally oversee your fittings. With her expertise in corsetry, Cadolle's custom lingerie proves that a perfect fit does more for your figure than any amount of dieting or treatments. At **Les Folies d'Elodie**, you can pick and choose colours or models from a tempting line of satin and hand-beaded sweet-nothings, while boudoir-like **Sabbia Rosa** can make to order models and sizes not in stock.

Bespoke for men

Made-to-measure is the key to many a French man's elegance, with a style that lies somewhere between British formality and Italian elan. Clothes obsessive John Malkovich famously chose a Paris tailor, before starting to design his own suits. With a name to match that of any of his aristocratic clients, Armand de Baudry d'Asson makes made-to-measure suits and shirts in the English-style at **A.B.A. Tailoring**.

With associations in France, Italy and Savile Row in London, Armand will conduct fittings at your work, home, or hotel; the end product is so sophisticated, you will wonder how you ever managed before.

For a balance between the English and Italian menswear styles, look no further than **Cifonelli**. **Charvet** on Place Vendôme is an institution famous the world over for its bespoke shirts, which require 18 different measurements; once painstakingly assembled, they are garments of absolute perfection. **Hilditch & Key** will do its traditionally tailored shirts for both men and women; Karl Lagerfeld has his own designs made up by this illustrious company, which has served the French aristocracy for decades. **Arnys** in Saint-Germain has been making made-to-measure suits and shirts since the 1930s, along with its famous *forestière* jackets. A more recent addition to the Parisian bespoke scene is **Eglé Bespoke**, which creates men's shirts and, a novelty until now, men's jeans! All will keep your measurements on file, so you needn't be shy about placing an order if it suddenly strikes your fancy during a business trip abroad.

Jewellery virtuosos

It's often the little touches that can make an outfit, so men in the know head to **Rosset-Gauléjac** for custom cufflinks and accessories. You will receive expert advice among a masculine mix of diamonds, enamel and gold. In the home of *haute jouaillerie*, Place Vendôme, visit **Laurenz Baumer** for his highly personalised approach. Baumer will accept a customer only after a lengthy interview, during which he does his utmost to learn about your tastes and desires; once initiated, he will cross the globe in his search for the ideal piece. **Antoine Chapoutot** is a very confidential address, based in a *hôtel particulier* on the Left Bank, while, just off avenue Montaigne, **Eternamé**, started by former Dior publicist Sarah Besnainou, has fashion crowds on either side of the Atlantic clamouring for her unique bespoke designs. Bearing a smaller price tag, **Inge Lex**'s adorable hand-beaded concoctions have a cult following in Japan.

03

Hats and gloves

Hats are still a necessary luxury in French high society, to be worn at weddings or special events like the Prix du Jockey Club and the Prix de Diane Hermès horse races. Well-known designers **Marie Mercié**, **Philippe Model** and **Jacques Le Corre** inevitably get an influx of orders around these summer events, so be certain to place yours in advance. Less known is **Isabelle Léourier**, who, after creating hats for the catwalks, now prefers one-off creations for individual clients, conceiving extravagant head ornaments like veritable sculptures.

Maison Massaro
2 rue de la Paix, 2nd

For men, the **Maison Motsch-Hermès** is the quintessential French *chapellerie*. Completing your total look, **Denise Francelle** is an invaluable source for gloves.

Shoes and leather goods

Well-heeled Parisiennes know **Delage** and the **Maison Massaro**, creators of the two-toned flat, by their history with the house of Chanel. **Repetto**, the now fashionable ballet shoe maker, will also construct made-to-measure models from its flagship store on rue de la Paix. Men's shoes are taken extremely seriously in France, with **Berluti** and **John Lobb** both heading their custom services from Paris. Pierre Corthay worked at both houses before starting his own luxury line, **Corthay,** in 1990. Family-run **Aubercy** has been crafting gentlemen's shoes since 1935, including an entirely made-to-measure *grande mésure* service, and has also added women's ballerinas and moccasins. Equestrians of both sexes look to the famous **Guibert** for their custom needs.

No Parisian outfit would be complete without a custom handbag, to place on the specially designed small chair provided by the highest class of restaurant. **Hermès** is probably best known for its Birkin and Kelly bags, which can be ordered in any skin, including exotics; **Serge Amoruso** concentrates on rarities; while three

Galerie Vérot-Dodat,
rue du Bouloi, 1st

generations at **Jean-Pierre Renard** have been lovingly customising handbags and other leather goods from their atelier in the Place du Palais Bourbon. The famous luxury luggage maker **Goyard** is enjoying a renaissance, and **Pinel et Pinel** has taken the idea of a luxury steamer trunk and transformed it into the ultimate high-tech accessory. For custom diaries, wallets, belts and watchstraps in every possible hue and skin visit the **Atelier du Bracelet Parisien. Duret** hand-stitches luggage, briefcases, purses and even cigar humidifiers to order.

Spectacle artisans

Both the short- and the long-sighted can make a fashion statement with their eyewear in Paris. Celebrities and the French literati trust **E.B. Meyrowitz** for custom glasses and optical needs. However, for handmade tortoiseshell frames you must call on **Maison Bonnet**. Christian Bonnet is the last great craftsman to perfect this craft. Stéphane Sarnin at **Histoire de Voir** is the specialist who does the leather eyewear and outré masks and visors for the fashion shows.

03

Perfume maestros

Few things are more evocative then scents, so commission your own special scent for a heady Parisian souvenir: **Francis Kurkdjian**, **Blaise Mautin** and **Parfums de Nicolaï** will transport your senses with their olfactory expertise. **Cartier**'s nose, Mathilde Laurent, will create the ultimate bespoke scent. Make an appointment with her at the rue de la Paix flagship to start the exacting process, which takes at least a year. It's a service also offered at **Maison Guerlain**, Guerlain's gorgeous Champs-Elysées flagship, but if you can't wait six months, the house will adapt a fragrance just for you from its exclusive Collection Privée. Complete your bespoke world with exclusive made-to-measure make-up created by Terry de Gunzburg at **by Terry**.

Haute couture

Alejandra di Andia
(by appointment)
5 r Marbeuf, 8th
Ⓜ George V
Ⓒ 01 40 70 97 38
alejandradiandia.com
⊕ 5/F7

Anne Hoguet
(by appointment)
2 bd de Strasbourg, 10th
Ⓜ Strasbourg St-Denis
Ⓒ 01 42 08 19 89
annehoguet.fr
⊕ 3-7/S5

Delphine Manivet
110 r du Cherche-Midi, 6th
Ⓜ Vaneau
Ⓒ 01 45 44 70 01
delphinemanivet.com
⊕ 10-14/K14

Dominique Sirop
(by appointment)
14 r du Fbg St-Honoré, 8th
Ⓜ Concorde
Ⓒ 01 42 66 60 57
dominiquesirop.com
⊕ 6/J7

E2 Chatenet
(by appointment)
15 r Martel, 10th
Ⓜ Château d'Eau
Ⓒ 01 47 70 15 14
e2-chatenet.com
⊕ 3-7/R5

Fanny Liautaud
13 r St-Florentin, 8th
Ⓜ Concorde
Ⓒ 01 42 86 82 84
fannyliautaud.com
⊕ 6/K8

Franck Sorbier Couture
(by appointment)
6 r J-Pierre Timbaud, 11th
Ⓜ Oberkampf
Ⓒ 01 42 38 02 14
francksorbier.com
⊕ 8/U8

Gérald Watelet
(by appointment)
62 r François 1er, 8th
Ⓜ George V
Ⓒ 01 43 59 49 00
geraldwatelet.com
⊕ 5/F7

Hervé L. Leroux
32 r Jacob
Ⓜ St-Germain-des-Prés
Ⓒ 01 55 42 00 39
⊕ 10/M12

J. Mendel
396 r St-Honoré, 1st
Ⓜ Concorde
Ⓒ 01 42 61 75 77
jmendel.com
⊕ 6/L8

Lanel
By appointment: 20 r des
Petits-Champs, 2nd
Ⓜ Pyramides
Ⓒ 01 42 97 52 20
regslanel.com
⊕ 7/N8

Legeron
(by appointment)
20 r des Petits-Champs, 2nd
Ⓜ Pyramides
Ⓒ 01 42 96 94 89
legeron.com
⊕ 7/N8

Lemarié
(by appointment)
103 r du Fbg St-Denis,
10th
Ⓜ Gare de l'Est
Ⓒ 01 47 70 02 45
✛ 7/R6

Maison Michel
(by appointment)
65 r Ste-Anne, 2nd
Ⓜ Quatre Septembre
Ⓒ 01 42 96 89 77
michel-paris.com
✛ 7/N8

Mercerie d'un Soir
37 r de Grenelle, 7th
Ⓜ Sèvres-Babylone
Ⓒ 01 45 48 26 13
✛ 10/L13

Lesage
(by appointment)
13 r de la Grange-
Batelière , 9th
Ⓜ Grands Boulevards
Ⓒ 01 44 79 00 88
✛ 7/O6

**Maurizio Galante
Interware**
(by appointment)
14 r d'Antin, 2nd
Ⓜ Opéra
Ⓒ 01 40 07 00 70
maurizio-galante.com
✛ 6/M7

Y de G
3rd floor, 40 cours
Albert 1er, 8th
Ⓜ Alma-Marceau
Ⓒ 01 53 75 00 07
y-de-g.com
✛ 5-6/G9

03

Lingerie supremos

Cadolle Couture
(by appointment)
255 r St-Honoré, 1st
Ⓜ Concorde
Ⓒ 01 42 60 94 94
cadolle.fr
✛ Off map

Les Folies d'Elodie
56 av Paul Doumer, 16th
Ⓜ Trocadéro
Ⓒ 01 45 04 93 57
netfolies.com
✛ 9/A10

Sabbia Rosa
73 r des Sts-Pères, 6th
Ⓜ St-Germain-des-Prés
Ⓒ 01 45 48 88 37
✛ 10/M11

Spectacle artisans

E. B. Meyrowitz
5 r de Castiglione, 1st
Ⓜ Tuileries
Ⓒ 01 42 60 63 64
meyrowitz.com
✛ 6/L8

Histoire de Voir
(by appointment)
8 passage de la Bonne-
Graine, 11th
Ⓜ Ledru-Rollin
Ⓒ 01 48 06 48 32
histoire-de-voir.com
✛ 12/W13

Maison Bonnet
(by appointment)
8 rue Tiphaine, 15th
Ⓜ Dupleix
Ⓒ 01 40 59 45 14
maisonbonnet.com
✛ 9-13/D14

Bespoke for men

A.B.A. Tailoring
(by appointment)
8 r St-Paul, 4th
Ⓜ St-Paul
ⓒ 01 42 72 07 18
mytailleur.com
⊕ 11-12/T13

Arnys
14 r de Sèvres, 7th
Ⓜ Sèvres Babylone
ⓒ 01 45 48 76 99
arnys.fr
⊕ 10-14/K14

Charvet
28 pl Vendôme, 1st
Ⓜ Opéra
ⓒ 01 42 60 30 70
⊕ 6/L8

Cifonelli
31 r Marbeuf, 8th
Ⓜ Franklin D. Roosevelt
ⓒ 01 42 25 38 84
⊕ 5/F7

Eglé Bespoke
26 r du Mont-Thabor, 1st
Ⓜ Tuileries
ⓒ 01 44 15 98 31
eglebespoke.com
⊕ 6/K8

Hilditch & Key
252 r de Rivoli, 1st
Ⓜ Tuileries
ⓒ 01 42 60 36 09
hilditchandkey.co.uk
⊕ 6/K8

Jewellery virtuosos

Antoine Chapoutot
12 r de Tournon, 6th
Ⓜ Odéon
ⓒ 01 43 26 47 76
chapoutot.com
⊕ 11-15/N14

Eternamé
5 r Clément-Marot, 8th
Ⓜ Alma-Marceau
ⓒ 01 40 69 08 00
⊕ 5/F8

Fleur Rozet
110 bd de Courcelles, 17th
Ⓜ Villiers
ⓒ 01 53 34 06 95
fleurrozet.com
⊕ 1-2/G3

Inge Lex
7 r du Pas-de-la-Mule, 4th
Ⓜ Chemin Vert
ⓒ 01 48 04 58 63
⊕ 12/U12

Laurenz Baumer
4 pl Vendôme, 1st
Ⓜ Opéra
ⓒ 01 42 86 99 33
lorenzbaumer.com
⊕ 6/l8

Rosset-Gauléjac
23 r Jacob, 6th
Ⓜ St-Germain des Prés
ⓒ 01 42 61 10 36
rosset-gaulejac.com
⊕ 10/M12

Hats and gloves

Denise Francelle
224 r de Rivoli, 1st
Ⓜ Tuileries
☎ 01 42 60 76 15
✛ 6/M9

Isabelle Léourier
(by appointment)
☎ 01 30 34 89 72
Isabelle-leourier.fr

Jacques Le Corre
193 r St-Honoré, 1st
Ⓜ Concorde
☎ 01 42 96 97 40
jacqueslecorre.com
✛ 6/L8

Maison Motsch-Hermès
42 av George V, 8th
Ⓜ George V
☎ 01 47 20 48 51
✛ 5/E7

Marie Mercié
23 r St-Sulpice, 6th
Ⓜ Mabillon
☎ 01 43 26 45 83
✛ 11/N13

Philippe Model
33 pl du Marché-St-
Honoré, 1st
Ⓜ Tuileries
☎ 01 42 96 89 02
✛ 6/M8

03

Perfume maestros

Blaise Mautin
(by appointment)
12 r d'Armaillé, 17th
Ⓜ Argentine
☎ 06 15 07 60 41
blaise-mautin.com
✛ 1/C4

By Terry
21 passage Véro-Dodat, 1st
Ⓜ Louvre Rivoli
☎ 01 44 76 00 76
byterry.com
✛ 7/O9

Cartier
13 r de la Paix, 2nd
Ⓜ Opéra
☎ 01 42 18 43 83
cartier.com
✛ 6/M7

Francis Kurkdjian
(by appointment)
17 r du Fbg St-Martin, 10th
Ⓜ Gare de l'Est
☎ 01 42 77 40 33
franciskurkdjian.com
✛ 3-4/T4

Maison Guerlain
68 av des Champs-
Elysées, 8th
Ⓜ Franklin D. Roosevelt
☎ 01 45 62 11 21
guerlain.com
✛ 6/H7

Parfums de Nicolaï
16 av Raymond
Poincaré, 16th
Ⓜ Trocadéro
☎ 01 47 55 90 44
pnicolai.com
✛ 5/B8

Shoes and leather goods

Atelier du Bracelet Parisien
7 r St-Hyacinthe, 1st
Ⓜ Tuileries
☏ 01 42 86 13 70
abp-paris.com
✠ 6/M8

Aubercy
34 r Vivienne, 2nd
Ⓜ Bourse
☏ 01 42 33 93 61
aubercy.com
✠ 7/O7

Berluti
26 r Marbeuf, 8th
Ⓜ Franklin D. Roosevelt
☏ 01 53 93 97 97
berluti.com
✠ 5/F7

Corthay
1 r Volney, 2nd
Ⓜ Opéra
☏ 01 42 61 08 89
corthay.fr
✠ 6/L7

Delage
159-161 galerie de
Valois, Jardin du Palais
Royal, 1st
Ⓜ Palais Royal
☏ 01 40 15 97 24
✠ 7/N8

Duret
29 r Duret, 16th
Ⓜ Argentine
☏ 01 40 67 93 05
duret-paris.com
✠ 1-5/B5

Goyard
233 r St-Honoré, 1st
Ⓜ Concorde
☏ 01 42 60 57 04
goyard.fr
✠ 6/L8

Guibert
22 av Victor-Hugo, 16th
Ⓜ Charles de Gaulle
- Etoile
☏ 01 53 64 74 74
guibert.fr
✠ 5/C6

Hermès
24 r du Fbg St-Honoré, 8th
Ⓜ Concorde
☏ 01 40 17 47 17
hermes.com
✠ 6/J7

Jean-Pierre Renard
3 pl du Palais Bourbon, 7th
Ⓜ Assemblée Nationale
☏ 01 45 51 77 87
renard-paris.com
✠ 10/J10

John Lobb
21 r Boissy d'Anglas, 8th
Ⓜ Madeleine
☏ 01 42 65 24 45
johnlobb.com
✠ 6/J7

Maison Massaro
2 r de la Paix , 2nd
Ⓜ Opéra
☏ 01 42 61 00 29
massaro.fr
✠ 6/M7

Pinel et Pinel
(by appointment)
5 r Cyrano de Bergerac, 18th
Ⓜ Jules Joffrin
☏ 01 45 23 11 14
pineletpinel.fr
✠ Off map

Repetto
22 r de la Paix, 2nd
Ⓜ Opéra
☏ 01 44 71 83 12
repetto.com
✠ 6/M7

Serge Amoruso
13 r Abel, 12th
Ⓜ Ledru-Rollin
☏ 01 43 45 14 10
sergeamoruso.com
✠ 16/W16

03

See page 9
to scan the
directory

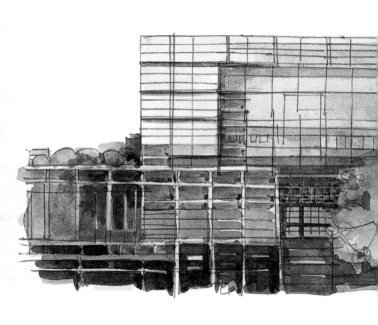

04

FASHIONABLE CULTURE
AND SMART ART

Musée des Arts Décoratifs and Musée de la Mode et du Textile
Palais du Louvre, 107 rue de Rivoli, 1st

Previous page: Fondation Cartier pour l'Art Contemporain
261 boulevard Raspail, 14th

Frequenting the right cultural venues is just as essential a part of the chic lifestyle as mastering the right dress codes. While the Louvre is fantastically comprehensive, replete with over 300,000 works of art, chic Parisian culture vultures are just as likely to be found at one-off exhibitions at one of the luxury-brand-sponsored foundations.

04

Fashionista chic

Rather than a single Victoria & Albert-style permanent collection, Paris has not one but two fashion museums that hold changing exhibitions, rotating their archives and benefitting from prestigious private loans. The **Musée Galliera** occupies a fanciful 19th-century *hôtel particulier* originally built to house the private collection of the Duchess of Galliera. The museum opens for two exhibitions a year, providing a stunning setting for wide-ranging retrospectives that have included "Marlene Dietrich, The Creation of a Legend" and "Paris Couture in the Thirties".

The **Musée de la Mode et du Textile**, part of the independently run decorative arts trio housed in a wing of the Louvre, mixes historical or textile-themed exhibitions with cutting-edge current design, such as the 2007 show curated by Christian Lacroix paying homage to fashion throughout the ages.

You can get even closer to haute couture at the **Fondation Pierre Bergé-Yves Saint Laurent**, a very select museum in the master's former atelier. Exhibitions alternate Yves Saint Laurent's most celebrated pieces with tributes to friends and inspirations. Space-age 60s minidresses by fellow stylist Pierre Cardin are the highlight of the **Musée Pierre Cardin**.

The **Musée Hermès** is a exclusive address, located above the Faubourg Saint-Honoré boutique, and open only by appointment to special customers. Meanwhile privileged clients of **Chaumet**, jeweller to Napolean, can visit its archive collection and salons that hosted Chopin. Also on Place Vendôme is the museum of luxury watchmaker **Bréguet**. Best time to visit is Tuesday when you are shown around by Emmanuel Bréguet.

Completing the fashion experience are Fragonard's **Musée du Parfum**, which offers an enjoyable glimpse into the history of scent, and the tiny **Musée de l'Eventail**, where amid historic and contemporary fans, you may see Anne Hoguet, who makes fans for haute couture designers, working away in her atelier.

Major art museums

The grand triumvirate of the **Louvre, Musée d'Orsay** and the **Centre Pompidou** will, between them, take you through the history of Western art from antiquity to the great Romantics (Louvre), via the high 19th century and Impressionists (Orsay) up to today (Pompidou) in three iconic buildings – royal palace, converted train station, high-tech pioneer – to match. Complete your Impressionist round-up with the unmissable Monets at the **Musée National de l'Orangerie** and the **Musée Marmottan-Claude Monet.** Non-Western art can be traced through the superb Asian art collections of the often-overlooked **Musée Guimet** and the eclectic tribal art displayed in the vast new **Musée du Quai Branly.**

04

Decorative arts museums

The **Musée des Arts Décoratifs** takes a thoroughly contemporary look at France's decorative arts prowess, though iconic furniture design from the Middle Ages to the 21st century. As well as Le Corbusier loungers and Pop Art bubble chairs, it has delicious tidbits like the painstakingly reconstructed 1920s suite of fashion designer Jeanne Lanvin. Its shop is a superb source of original design items and jewels.

Espace Louis Vuitton
60 rue de Bassano, 8th

Luxury houses whose archive collections are available for viewing include the **Galerie-Musée Baccarat**, the **Musée Puiforcat** and **Bouilhet-Christofle Musée d'Orfèvrerie**, the latter located amid the buildings in Saint Denis, where Christofle has produced silverware since 1874. Pierre Cardin's personal collection of Majorelle, Tiffany and other Art Nouveau items can be seen, arranged as if in a courtesan's apartment, at **La Collection 1900** above Maxim's restaurant. Visits must be reserved ahead and can be combined with lunch in Maxim's splendid Art Nouveau dining room.

04

A remarkable testament to the forgotten craft of tapestry, in which France was the world leader, the **Galerie des Gobelins** reopened in May 2007 after 35 years of renovation. Works on show span four centuries; the earliest is *Tenture d'Artémise*, commissioned by Henri IV in 1607. You'll be amazed by the delicate handwork and mystical appeal of these subtle masterpieces.

Lifestyle collections

If you hanker after times gone by, immerse yourself in lost elegance at the **Musée Nissim de Camondo**, an astonishing collection of 18th-century decorative arts in a private mansion modelled on the Petit Trianon at Versailles. Beyond the grand reception rooms,

Galerie des Gobelins
42 avenue des Gobelins, 13th

the bedrooms, bathrooms and kitchens recapture the lifestyle of a French Jewish family who perished at Auschwitz. Another sumptuous residence is the **Musée Jacquemart-André**, built for wealthy aesthetes and collectors Edouard André and Nélie Jacquemart for treasures that include Italian Renaissance paintings, and French and Dutch Old Masters. You can also lunch or tea in the very chic café under a ceiling painted by Tiepolo. In the Marais, the **Musée Cognacq-Jay** is laid out as a series of panelled period rooms to house the Fragonards, Chardins, Guardi and Canaletto, fine 18th-century furniture and *objets d'art* amassed by the founder of La Samaritaine department store.

Elegant exhibition spaces

A real style favourite, the **Fondation Cartier** hosts quirky, original exhibitions of contemporary art, often crossing the boundaries into other disciplines, such as a David Lynch retrospective. The opening parties in the glass-walled Jean Nouvel building are not to be missed. **Maison Rouge** is a private foundation which allows the rare privilege of seeing the works amassed by private collectors. The late opening hours (until midnight) attract a smart west Parisian set to the **Palais de Tokyo**, though as much for its restaurant, Tokyo Eat, as for its dynamic exhibitions.

04

Not to be outdone, the **Espace Louis Vuitton** is a cultural destination on the top floor of Vuitton's Champs-Elysées boutique, which has shown artists like Vanessa Beecroft and Nicolas Moulin. It's a mere hint of the shows to come in the future Louis Vuitton Foundation for Creation, due to open in 2010 in an extraordinary building designed by Frank Gehry, in the Jardin d'Acclimatation in the Bois de Boulogne.

Commercial art galleries

Commercial galleries are an essential part of the Parisian cultural arena and act as a necessary means of discovering and supporting new talent. The heart of the contemporary gallery scene is in the Marais and adjoining Beaubourg. Designer Agnès b exhibits a great balance of established and emerging talents at **Galerie du Jour Agnès b**, while **Galerie Chez Valentin**, **Emmanuel Perrotin** and **Thaddaeus Ropac** are all popular with the chic crowd. On smart avenue Matignon, **Galerie Jérôme de Noirmont** attracts *le beau monde* with contemporary artists like Bettina Rheims, Pierre & Gilles, and the drop-dead stylish, Anh Duong. **Air de Paris** heads a group of younger galleries on rue Louise-Weiss, near the Bibliothèque Nationale François Mitterrand in the under-construction 13th *arrondissement*, and attracts an edgy fashion crowd to photographic exhibitions by the likes of Inez van Lamsweerde and Vinoodh Matadin.

Antiques and modern design galleries

Brothers Nicolas and Alexis Kugel count Hubert de Givenchy among their clients at **Galerie J. Kugel**, a fabulous emporium of museum-worthy antique furnishings located in the sumptuous neo-classical Hôtel Côllot. Other antique dealers abound near here in the area dubbed the Carré Rive Gauche, bordered by the quai Voltaire, rue des Saints Pères, rue du Bac and rue de l'Université, where **Stéphane Olivier** is an inexhaustible source of unusual lamps, antique statuary, architectural effects and other curios. Nearby in Saint-Germain, **Vallois** leads the way in Art Deco glamour for the serious collector. Across the Seine, Pierre Passebon indulges in his penchant for 20th-century furnishings at the **Galerie du Passage** in the historic Galerie Véro-Dodat, where you will find treasures by Jean Royère and Piero Fornasetti, among others, while **Galerie Alexis Lahellec** focuses on the sophisticated minimalism of 1960s Scandinavian design. To keep right up to date, check out the current generation of hip international designers on show at **Galerie Kréo** in the 13th and the finely crafted art pottery at **Carlin Gallery** in Saint-Germain.

04

A phenomenon that has had a great deal of success is the fashion or jewellery gallery, such as **Joyce,** launched by stylish Joyce Ma, where designers, photographers and artists from or influenced by Asia are exhibited. **Galerie Naïla de Monbrison** presents work by jewellery artists such as Tina Chow and Gilles Jonemann from her exclusive location on the Left Bank. In addition to flamboyant antique costume jewellery, **Sylvie Corbelin** also sells her own original designs at the Puces de Saint-Ouen fleamarket, with a second outlet in Bon Marché department store. Visit **Galerie Hélène Porée** to discover its unique roster of jewellery talents, and **Ibu Gallery** at Palais Royal, where jewellery is exhibited alongside vases and furniture.

Musée National Rodin
77 rue de Varenne, 7th

DIRECTORY FASHIONABLE CULTURE AND SMART ART

Fashionista chic

**Fondation Pierre Bergé
Yves Saint-Laurent**
1 r Léonce Reynaud, 16th
Ⓜ Alma Marceau
Ⓒ 01 44 31 64 00
ysl-hautecouture.com
✛ 5/E8

Musée de l'Eventail
2 bd de Strasbourg, 10th
Ⓜ Strasbourg St Denis
Ⓒ 01 42 08 19 89
annehoguet.fr
✛ 3-7/S5

**Musée de la Mode
et du Textile**
Palais du Louvre,
107 r de Rivoli, 1st
Ⓜ Palais Royal
Ⓒ 01 44 55 57 50
lesartsdecoratifs.fr
✛ 6/M9

Musée Bréguet
6 pl Vendôme, 1st
Ⓜ Opéra
Ⓒ 01 47 03 65 00
breguet.com
✛ 6/L6

Musée Galliera
Palais Galliera,
10 av Pierre 1er de
Serbie, 16th
Ⓜ Iéna
Ⓒ 01 56 52 86 00
galliera.paris.fr
✛ 5/E8

Musée du Parfum
9 r Scribe, 9th
Ⓜ Opéra
Ⓒ 01 47 42 04 56
fragonard.com
✛ 6/L6

Musée Chaumet
12 pl Vendôme, 1st
Ⓜ Opéra
Ⓒ 01 44 77 26 26
chaumet.com
✛ 6/L8

Musée Hermès
24 Fbg St-Honoré, 8th
Ⓜ Concorde
01 40 17 47 17
hermes.com
✛ 6/J7

Musée Pierre Cardin
35 bd Victor Hugo,
St-Ouen
Ⓜ Mairie de Clichy
Ⓒ 01 40 11 21 48
pierrecardin.com
✛ Off map

04

Commercial art galleries

Air de Paris
32 r Louise Weiss, 13th
Ⓜ Chevaleret
Ⓒ 01 44 23 02 77
airdeparis.com
⊕ Off map

Galerie Emmanuel Perrotin
76 r de Turenne, 3rd
Ⓜ St Sébastien Froissart
Ⓒ 01 42 16 79 79
galerieperrotin.com
⊕ 10-14/M14

Galerie Thaddaeus Ropac
7 r Debelleyme, 3rd
Ⓜ St-Sébastien-Froissart
Ⓒ 01 42 72 99 00
ropac.net
⊕ 7-8/T10

Galerie Chez Valentin
9 r St-Gilles, 3rd
Ⓜ Chemin Vert
Ⓒ 01 48 87 42 55
galeriechezvalentin.com
⊕ 12/U11

Galerie du Jour Agnès b
44 r Quincampoix, 4th
Ⓜ Rambuteau
Ⓒ 01 44 54 55 90
galeriedujour.com
⊕ 7/9

Jérôme de Noirmont
38 av Matignon, 8th
Ⓜ Franklin D Roosevelt
Ⓒ 01 42 89 89 00
denoirmont.com
⊕ 6/H7

Elegant exhibition spaces

Espace Louis Vuitton
60 r de Bassano, 8th
Ⓜ George V
Ⓒ 01 53 57 52 03
louisvuitton.com
⊕ Off ma

Galeries Nationales du Grand Palais
3 av du Général-Eisenhower, 8th
Ⓜ Champs-Elysées-Clemenceau
Ⓒ 01 41 57 32 28
rmn.fr
⊕ 6/H8

Musée du Luxembourg
19 r de Vaugirard, 6th
Ⓡ Luxembourg
Ⓒ 01 42 34 25 95
museeduluxembourg.fr
⊕ 10-14/M14

Fondation Cartier pour l'Art Contemporain
261 bd Raspail, 14th
Ⓜ Raspail
Ⓒ 01 42 18 56 50
fondation.cartier.fr
⊕ 14/L17

La Maison Rouge-Fondation Antoine de Galbert
10 bd de la Bastille, 12th
Ⓜ Quai de la Rapée
Ⓒ 040 01 08 81.
lamaisonrouge.org
⊕ 5/E6

Palais de Tokyo Site de Création contemporaine
13 av du Pdt-Wilson, 16th
Ⓜ Iéna
Ⓒ 01 47 23 38 86
palaisdetokyo.com
⊕ 5/C9

Major art museums

Centre Pompidou
r St-Martin, 4th
Ⓜ Hôtel de Ville
Ⓒ 01 44 78 12 33
centrepompidou.fr
⊕ 11/R10

Musée Marmottan-Claude Monet
2 r Louis-Boilly, 16th
Ⓜ Ranelagh.
Ⓒ 01 44 96 50 33
marmottan.com
⊕ Off map

Musée National Rodin
Hôtel Biron, 77 r de Varenne, 7th
Ⓜ Varenne
Ⓒ 01 44 18 61 10
musee-rodin.fr
⊕ 10/I12

Musée Guimet
6 pl d'Iéna, 16th
Ⓜ Iéna
Ⓒ 01 56 52 53 00
museeguimet.fr
⊕ 5/D9

Musée National de l'Orangerie
Jardin des Tuileries, 1st
Ⓜ Concorde
Ⓒ 01 40 20 67 71
musee-orangerie.fr
⊕ 6/L9

Musée d'Orsay
1 r de la Légion d'Honneur, 7th
Ⓜ Solférino
Ⓒ 01 40 49 48 14
musee-orsay.fr
⊕ 10/K10

04

Musée du Louvre
99 r de Rivoli, 1st
Ⓜ Palais-Royal
Ⓒ 01 40 20 53 17
louvre.fr
⊕ 6/M9

Musée National Picasso
Hôtel Salé, 5 r de Thorigny, 3rd
Ⓜ St-Paul
Ⓒ 01 42 71 25 21
musee-picasso.fr
⊕ 11-12/T10

Musée du Quai Branly
37 quai Branly, 7th
Ⓜ Alma-Marceau
Ⓒ 01 56 61 72 72
quaibranly.fr
⊕ 9/E10

Lifestyle collections

Musée Cognacq-Jay
8 r Elzévir, 3rd
Ⓜ St-Paul
Ⓒ 01 40 27 07 21
cognacq-jay.paris.fr
⊕ 11-12/T11

Musée Jacquemart-Andre
158 bd Haussmann, 8th
Ⓜ Miromesnil
Ⓒ 01 45 62 11 59
musee-jacquemart-andre.com
⊕ 2-6/I5

Musée Nissim de Camondo
63 r de Monceau, 8th
Ⓜ Monceau
Ⓒ 01 53 89 06 50
lesartsdecoratifs.fr
⊕ 2/H4

Joyce
168-173 galerie de Valois, 1st

Decorative arts museums

Bouilhet-Christofle Musée d'Orfèvrerie
112 r Ambroise Croizat,
St-Denis
Ⓜ St Denis
Ⓒ 01 49 22 40 40
christofle.com
✪ Off map

Galerie des Gobelins
42 av des Gobelins, 13th
Ⓜ Gobelins
Ⓒ 01 44 08 53 49
mobiliernational.culture.
gouv.fr
✪ Off map

Musée des Arts Décoratifs
Palais du Louvre,
107 r de Rivoli, 1st
Palais Royal
Ⓒ 01 44 55 57 50
lesartsdecoratifs.fr
✪ 6/M9

La Collection 1900
Maxim's, 3 r Royale, 8th
Ⓜ Concorde
Ⓒ 01 42 65 30 47
maxims-musee.
artnouveau.com
✪ 6/K7

Galerie Musée Baccarat
11 pl des Etats Unis, 16th
Ⓜ Boissière
Ⓒ 01 40 22 11 00
baccarat.fr
✪ 5/D7

Musée Puiforcat
48 av Gabriel, 8th
Ⓜ Franklin D Roosevelt
Ⓒ 01 45 63 10 10
puiforcat.com
✪ 6/H7

Antiques and modern design galleries

Carlin Gallery
93 r de Seine, 6th
Ⓜ Mabillon
ⓒ 01 44 07 39 54
⊕ 11/N12

Galerie Alexis Lahellec
16 r Jean-Jacques
Rousseau, 1st
Ⓜ Palais Royal
ⓒ 01 42 33 36 95
alexislahellec.com
⊕ 7/O9

Galerie Hélène Porée
1 r de l'Odéon, 6th
Ⓜ Odéon
ⓒ 01 43 54 17 00
galerie-helene-poree.com
⊕ 11/N13

Galerie J. Kugel
25 quai Anatole France,
7th
Ⓜ Assemblée-Nationale
ⓒ 01 42 60 86 23
galerie-kugel.com
⊕ 10/L10

Galerie Kréo
22 r Duchefdelaville, 13th
Ⓜ Chevaleret
ⓒ 01 53 60 18 42
galeriekreo.com
⊕ Off map

Galerie Naïla de Monbrison
6 r de Bourgogne, 7th
Ⓜ Assemblée Nationale
ⓒ 01 47 05 11 15
⊕ 10/I11

Galerie du Passage
20-22 galerie Véro-Dodat, 1st
Ⓜ Louvre Rivoli
ⓒ 01 42 36 01 13
galeriedupassage.com
⊕ 7/O9

Ibu Gallery
162 galerie de Valois, 1st
Ⓜ Palais Royal
ⓒ 01 42 60 06 41
⊕ 7/N9

Joyce
168-173 galerie de
Valois, 1st
Ⓜ Palais Royal
ⓒ 01 40 15 03 72
⊕ 7/N9

Stéphane Olivier
3 r de l'Université, 7th
Ⓜ St Germain des Prés
ⓒ 01 42 96 10 00
stephaneolivier.fr
⊕ 10/L11

04

Sylvie Corbelin
Marché Paul Bert,
110 r de Rosiers,
93400 St Ouen
Ⓜ Porte de Clignancourt
ⓒ 06 07 76 41 13
sylvie-corbelin.com
⊕ Off map

Vallois
35, 41 r de Seine, 6th
Ⓜ Mabillon
ⓒ 01 43 29 50 84
vallois.com
⊕ 11/N12

See page 9
to scan the
directory

LADUREE

RESTAURANTS, CAFES
AND TEAROOMS

Le Grand Véfour
17 rue de Beaujolais, 1st

Previous page: Ladurée
16 rue Royale, 8th

When Paris became the place to buy your fashion, it needed suitably stylish establishments to host the avid foreign shoppers. This is how the city's tradition of *hôtellerie* and haute cuisine restaurants evolved. Paris offers some of the world's most extravagant dining experiences. Haute cuisine chefs cluster in a mini-galaxy here, in establishments where the splendid cuisine is often matched by equally magnificent historical decor. The influence trickles down through top chefs's own more modest restaurants to the modern bistros that have made an art of updating French classics with contemporary touches. But in this fashion capital, eating out can also mean who, rather than what, is being served up at the handful of addresses that act like a dining club for the A-list when they are in town.

05

Decadent dining

With a sweep through double doors into a palatial dining room hung with chandeliers like a cloud of tiny water droplets, the theatre begins at **Alain Ducasse**. This master chef offers the ultimate luxury dining experience at the Plaza Athénée, where you can choose between a truffle and crustacean-led blow-out, or the more demure Pleasures of the Table menu. The true palace experience awaits under an angel-painted ceiling in the dining room of **Le Meurice**, where chef Yannick Alléno has wittily reinvigorated classic cuisine. One of Paris's oldest restaurants, the 18th-century **Le Grand Véfour**, is reminiscent of the Palais Royal's days as a pleasure garden. Amid mirrors and painted panels, Guy Martin serves up his impeccable haute cuisine. In the heart of the Bois de Boulogne **Le Pré Catelan** enchants diners with its Napoléon III decor and a summer terrace in a rose garden. Chef Frédéric Anton has pared down his cuisine to make the ingredients king, as has Alain Passard at **L'Arpège**, where even humble carrots and beetroot, garnered from an exclusive kitchen garden, become stars on his menu.

At **Apicius**, chef Jean-Pierre Vigato's cooking is directly inspired by the eponymous food writer of ancient Rome, and served in a contemporary dining room in an 18th-century *hôtel particulier*, while for wine lovers there is no greater restaurant than the esteemed classic **Taillevent**. For gourmets in search of new taste sensations, it is avant-garde **Pierre Gagnaire** who will delight. Molecular biology holds the key to cuisine that boldly goes where no chef has gone before.

Rooms with a view

For decadence inspired by a dream setting, **Maison Blanche** on avenue Montaigne tops the list. This restaurant by the Pourcel twins of Montpellier offers Mediterranean dining in a swish white, minimalist penthouse with the whole panorama of Paris spread below. At **Les Ombres**, on top of the new Musée du Quai Branly, you dine under the stars on its panoramic terrace, tasting the multi-course *menu gastronomique* delicately spiced with flavours from exotic lands.

The ultimate table to book for a hot date must be on the terrace of **Café de l'Homme** in the Palais de Chaillot, an impossibly chic restaurant run by media darling Coco Couperie. The Eiffel Tower is so near you can almost touch it, while inside long tubular chandeliers give the sultry setting a glamorous glow. Flirt with the dark side at **Black Calvados**, where an 18th-century painted ceiling and a nebuchadnezzar of Champagne cry "decadence" in the midst of a room entirely painted black. Beware the loud music, though, this is rock hedonism at its most extreme.

Georges, atop the Centre Pompidou, is a perennial fashion favourite for its lean cuisine, immaculate staff, whose looks rival those of the models who eat here, and fabulous views of the Paris skyline.

05

Le Voltaire
27 quai Voltaire, 7th

Intimate atmospheres

Where in Paris can a man entertain his mistress, or a lady her paramour, in total privacy? At **Lapérouse**, a gastronomic destination that began its life in 1766, both the restaurant and the private salons are still intact, and although the food has had its ups and downs, the exquisite setting remains a fashion world favourite – both John Galliano and Miucia Prada have held private dinners here. Another hideaway is **1728**, a magnificent historic mansion once inhabited by General Lafayette, where panelled salons follow each other in enfilade. For your tête-à-tête, request the Cabinet des Amateurs, a private, 12-square-metre room with a purple colour scheme.

05

Staying with period splendour, **L'Ambroisie** is housed in two beautiful, candlelit salons on Place des Vosges, providing an elegant setting for Bernard Pacaud's truffle-rich cuisine. At the fashionable Philippe Starck-designed **Cristal Room** in the Maison Baccarat you can reserve the private salon with a black chandelier. For a refined, quiet setting that does justice to one of Paris's finest chefs, choose **Hiramatsu**, where the Japanese balance and grace meet French haute cuisine.

Perfume specialist Frédéric Malle calls **Le Voltaire** the "most grown-up jet-set bistro in Paris," – but what's lovely about it is that everybody is greeted with equal warmth by maître d'Antoine. For a modern take on French cuisine, try **Spring**. American chef Daniel Rose welcomes a maximum of 16 guests serving up his daily menu as if giving a dinner party for friends.

Fashionable dining

Fashionistas in Paris for the shows tend to stick to the same time-honoured addresses, but having the number in your black book is one thing and getting a table is quite another. At Chinese restaurant **Davé** you can forget it if you haven't been featured in American *Vogue*, whose editor, Anna Wintour, hosted photographer Helmut Newton's memorial service here. **Chez Omar** is run by the affable Omar himself and once he knows your name, you're in. Until then keep queuing up for his delicious North African fare.

Tom Ford has hosted friends, including Gwyneth Paltrow, at **Caviar Kaspia**, while sushi addicts head to **Kinugawa** for a Tokyo flashback. The organic Italian food found at **Cibus** is a favourite of Sophia Coppola, and **L'Avenue** on avenue Montaigne is every fashion editor's between-shows canteen. Other popular fashion haunts include the enduringly hip restaurant at the **Hôtel Costes; Mathis;** and **L'Etoile**, with its dining room overlooking the Arc de Triomphe and glitzy basement dance floor.

Great chefs' spin-offs

Weary of catering only to the very rich, Paris's super-chefs have been branching out with dressed-down restaurants where the food is more accessible. Ducasse began expanding his empire with **Spoon Food & Wine**, which opened in 1998 with its revolutionary (at least in rule-bound France) formula, allowing you to make your own choice of sauces and accompaniments. He has also lent his magic touch to two traditional bistros, **Aux Lyonnais** and **Benoît**.

Guy Savoy's empire is nearly as dense – his **Les Bouquinistes** is a modern favourite in Saint-Germain. **L'Atelier de Joël Robuchon** is communal dining at its most chic, allowing customers to observe the preparation of their meals or taste a multitude of tapas-size portions; Hélène Darroze does a similar thing at **Le Salon d'Hélène**.

Guy Martin and Pierre Gagnaire are both clearly aiming to woo a younger crowd with **Sensing** and **Gaya par Pierre Gagnaire**, respectively, where sharp contemporary decor and creativity on the plate (in Gagnaire's case, principally with fish) are the order of the day. At the **Rôtisserie du Beaujolais**, an offshoot of La Tour d'Argent, you'll eat the best roast chicken with mashed potato in town.

05

Le Pré Verre
8 rue Thénard, 5th

Chic lunch spots

While taking the good-value lunch menus at haute cuisine establishments is the perfect way to enjoy this deluxe experience for less, lunch often calls for less opulent surroundings. The perfect place for a power lunch is **Chiberta**, one of Guy Savoy's offshoots, with resolutely masculine black and red décor and the chance to sit at the bar if you wish. Top chef Michel Rostang's daughter Caroline runs **L'Absinthe**, one of many restaurants patronised by bankers and chic shoppers in the Marché Saint-Honoré, and it has an attractive terrace. Inventive modern fare with Asian influences comes from William Ledeuil at his hip bistro **Ze Kitchen Galerie**, focusing on meat and fish grilled *a la plancha*, while the huge plate of antipasti at **Café Baci** makes for a perfect light lunch at Christian Lacroix's local canteen in the Marais.

05

The antipasti and *grandes salades* are also delicious at **Café Marly** and **Café de l'Esplanade**. These prime terrace spots are both part of the Costes brothers's empire, the former overlooking the Louvre pyramid and the latter the formal gardens of Les Invalides. Other excellent summer terrace options include gastronomic **Laurent**, in the shadows of the Elysées Palace, **Drouant** and the Gérard Depardieu-owned **Fontaine Gaillon**, both on peaceful Place Gaillon near Opéra. For a bargain

Alain Ducasse at the Plaza Athénée
25 avenue Montaigne, 8th

set menu in a buzzy bistro atmosphere plump for **Le Pré Verre**, the haunt of chic Latin Quarter inhabitants and academics from the nearby Sorbonne university. But if it's one of those days when only a steak-frites will do, follow the beau monde to **Relais de Venise**, which serves only that.

Tea and cake

The tinkling of teaspoons on china cups has been heard in Paris since the British stopped here in preparation for the Grand Tour. **Angelina**, near the Hôtel Meurice, has all the Maggie Smith appeal of this era, with its columns and suited waiters, and despite its fame delivers a satisfying afternoon tea or hot chocolate to a mixture of tourists and Hermès-scarfed Parisiennes.

The most glamorous tea salon of all is the ethereal Galerie des Gobelins in the **Plaza Athénée**, from whose cushioned chairs you can watch the fashion world glide by. Former Chanel muse Inès de La Fressange always cites **Ladurée** as one of her little pleasures. The original rue Royale branch is the most delightful, with its angel-painted ceiling, and you can take a bit of it home with you in the form of delectable macaroons. For young Parisians who've done their stint in South Ken, however, there is currently nothing more chic than the oh-so-British apple crumble, which is available, along with scones and mugs of tea, at **Rose Bakery** in the smart and foodie rue des Martyrs.

05

Decadent dining

Alain Ducasse
Hôtel Plaza Athénée
25 av Montaigne, 8th
Ⓜ Alma-Marceau
Ⓒ 01 53 67 65 00
alain-ducasse.com
⊕ 5/F8

Les Ambassadeurs
Hôtel de Crillon, 10 pl de
la Concorde, 8th
Ⓜ Concorde
Ⓒ 01 44 71 16 16
crillon.com
⊕ 6/J8

Apicius
20 r d'Artois, 8th
Ⓜ St Philippe du Roule
Ⓒ 01 43 20 19 66
⊕ 5-6/G6

L'Arpège
84 r de Varenne, 7th
Ⓜ Varenne
Ⓒ 01 45 51 47 33
alain-passard.com
⊕ 10/I12

Astrance
4 r Beethoven, 16th
Ⓜ Passy
Ⓒ 01 40 50 84 40
⊕ 9/B11

Le Grand Véfour
17 r de Beaujolais, 1st
Ⓜ Palais Royal
Ⓒ 01 42 96 56 27
relaischateaux.com/vefour
⊕ 7/N8

Le Jules Verne
Eiffel Tower, Champ-de-
Mars, 7th
Ⓜ Bir Hakeim
Ⓒ 01 45 55 61 44
⊕ 9/D11

Le Meurice
Hôtel Meurice,
228 r de Rivoli, 1st
Ⓜ Tuileries
Ⓒ 01 44 58 10 55
lemeurice.com
⊕ 6/M9

Le Pré Catelan
Route de Suresnes, Bois de
Boulogne, 16th
Ⓜ Porte Dauphiné
Ⓒ 01 44 14 41 14
precatelanparis.com
⊕ Off map

Pierre Gagnaire
6 r Balzac, 8th
Ⓜ George V
Ⓒ 01 58 36 12 50
pierre-gagnaire.com
⊕ 5/E6

La Table du Lancaster
Hospes Lancaster, 7 r du
Berri, 8th
Ⓜ George V
Ⓒ 01 40 76 40 18
hotel-lancaster.fr
⊕ 5/F6

Taillevent
15 r Lamennais, 8th
Ⓜ George V
Ⓒ 01 44 95 15 01
taillevent.com
⊕ 1-5/F5

Rooms with a view

Benkay
Novotel Paris Tour Eiffel,
61 quai de Grenelle, 15th
Ⓜ Bir-Hakeim
Ⓒ 01 40 58 21 26
⊕ 9/B13

Black Calvados
40 av Pierre 1er de Serbie, 8th
Ⓜ George V
Ⓒ 01 47 20 77 77
⊕ 5/E8

Café de l'Homme
17 pl du Trocadéro, 16th
Ⓜ Trocadéro
Ⓒ 01 44 05 30 15
cafedelhomme.com
⊕ 5/B9

Georges
6th floor, Centre
Pompidou,19 r
Beaubourg, 4th
Ⓜ Rambuteau
Ⓒ 01 44 78 47 99
⊕ 11/R10

Maison Blanche
15 av Montaigne, 8th
Ⓜ Alma Marceau
Ⓒ 01 47 23 55 99
maison-blanche.fr
⊕ 5/F8

Les Ombres
Musée du Quai Branly, 7th
Ⓜ Alma-Marceau
Ⓒ 01 47 53 68 00
lesombres-restaurant.com
⊕ 9/E10

Fashionable dining

L'Avenue
41 av Montaigne, 8th
Ⓜ Alma-Marceau
Ⓒ 01 40 70 14 91
⊕ 5/F8

Davé
12 r de Richelieu, 1st
Ⓜ Palais Royal
Ⓒ 01 42 61 49 48
⊕ 7/N9

Kinugawa
9 r du Mont-Thabor, 1st
Ⓜ Tuileries
Ⓒ 01 42 60 65 07
⊕ 6/K8

Caviar Kaspia
17 pl de la Madeleine, 8th
Ⓜ Madeleine
Ⓒ 01 42 65 33 32
kaspia.fr
⊕ 6/K7

L'Etoile
12 r de Presbourg, 16th
Ⓜ Charles de Gaulle
Etoile
Ⓒ 01 45 00 78 70
l-etoile.com
⊕ 1-5/C5

Kong
1 r du Pont Neuf
Ⓜ Pont Neuf
Ⓒ 01 40 39 09 00
kong.fr
⊕ 11/P10

05

Chez Omar
47 r de Bretagne, 3rd
Ⓜ Temple
Ⓒ 01 42 72 36 26
⊕ 7-8/T9

Hôtel Costes
239 r St-Honoré, 1st
Ⓜ Tuileries
Ⓒ 01 42 44 50 25
hotelcostes.com
⊕ 6/L8

Mathis
3 r de Ponthieu, 8th
Ⓜ Champs Elysées
Clemenceau
Ⓒ 01 42 25 73 01
⊕ 5-6/G6

Cibus
6 r Molière, 1st
Ⓜ Palais Royal
Ⓒ 01 42 61 50 19
⊕ 7/N8

Kai
18 r du Louvre, 1st
Ⓜ Louvre Rivoli
Ⓒ 01 40 15 04 99
⊕ 7/O9

Mori Venice Bar
2 r du Quatre
Septembre, 2nd
Ⓜ Bourse
Ⓒ 01 44 55 51 55
mori-venicebar
⊕ 7/O7

Intimate dining

1728
8 r d'Anjou, 8th
Ⓜ Concorde
Ⓒ 01 40 17 04 77
restaurant-1728.com
⊕ 6/J6

L'Ambroisie
9 pl des Vosges, 4th
Ⓜ Bastille
Ⓒ 01 42 78 51 45
ambroisie-place
desvosges.com
⊕ 12/U12

Cristal Room
Maison Baccarat, 11 pl des
Etats-Unis, 16th
Ⓜ Boissière
Ⓒ 01 40 22 11 10
baccarat.fr
⊕ 5/D7

Le Clyde
4 r du Mail, 2nd
Ⓜ Tuileries
Ⓒ 01 40 20 40 04
⊕ 7/O8

L'Epi Dupin
11 r Dupin, 6th
Ⓜ Sèvres Babylone
Ⓒ 01 42 22 64 56
⊕ 10-14/K14

Ferdi
32 r du Mont Thabor, 1st
Ⓜ Concorde
Ⓒ 01 42 6 82 52
⊕ 6/K8

Hiramatsu
52 r de Longchamp, 16th
Ⓜ Trocadéro
Ⓒ 01 56 81 08 80
hiramatsu.co.jp/fr
⊕ 5/B8

Lapérouse
51 quai des Grands-
Augustins, 6th
Ⓜ St-Michel
Ⓒ 01 43 26 90 14
restaurantlaperouse.com
⊕ 11/O12

Rosito
4 r du Pas de la Mule, 4th
Ⓜ St Paul
Ⓒ 01 42 76 04 44
⊕ 12/U12

Spring
28 r de La Tour
d'Auvergne, 9th
Ⓜ Pigalle
Ⓒ 01 45 96 05 72
⊕ 3/O3

Le Timbre
3 r Ste Beuve, 6th
Ⓜ Vavin
Ⓒ 01 45 49 10 40
⊕ 14/L16

Le Voltaire
27 quai Voltaire, 7th
Ⓜ Rue du Bac
01 42 61 17 49
⊕ 10/M11

L'Atelier de Joël Robuchon
5 r Montalembert, 7th
Ⓜ Rue du Bac
Ⓒ 01 42 22 56 56
joel-robuchon.com
✛ 10/L11

Aux Lyonnais
32 r St-Marc, 2nd
Ⓜ Bourse
Ⓒ 01 42 96 65 04
alain-ducasse.com
✛ 7/N7

Benoît
20 r St-Martin, 4th
Ⓜ Rambuteau
Ⓒ 01 42 72 25 76
alain-ducasse.com
✛ 7/R9

Les Bouquinistes
53 quai des Grands-Augustins, 6th
Ⓜ St-Michel
Ⓒ 01 43 25 45 94
lesbouquinistes.com
✛ 11/O12

Gaya par Pierre Gagnaire
44 r du Bac, 7th
Ⓜ Rue du Bac
Ⓒ 01 45 44 73 73
pierre-gagnaire.com
✛ 10/K1

Rôtisserie du Beaujolais
19 quai de la Tournelle, 5th
Ⓜ Cardinal Lemoine
Ⓒ 01 43 54 17 47
✛ 11-15/R14

Le Salon d'Hélène
4 r d'Assas, 6th
Ⓜ Sèvres Babylone
Ⓒ 01 42 22 00 11
✛ 10-14/L14

Sensing
19 r Bréa, 6th
Ⓜ Vavin
01 43 27 08 80
✛ 6/L6

Spoon Food & Wine
14 r de Marignan, 8th
Ⓜ Franklin D Roosevelt
Ⓒ 01 40 76 34 44
spoon.tm.fr
✛ 5-6/G7

05

Tea and cakes

Angelina
226 r de Rivoli, 1st
Ⓜ Tuileries
Ⓒ 01 42 60 82 00
✛ 6/L8

Ladurée
75 av des Chps-Elysées, 8th
Ⓜ Georges V
Ⓒ 01 40 75 08 75
✛ 5/F6

Rose Bakery
46 r des Martyrs, 9th
Ⓜ N D de Lorette
Ⓒ 01 42 82 12 80
✛ Off map

Le Grand Véfour
17 rue de Beaujolais, 1st

chic lunch spots

L'Absinthe
26 pl du Marché
St-Honoré, 1st
Ⓜ Tuileries
Ⓒ 01 49 26 90 04
⊕ 6/M8

Café Baci
36 r de Turenne, 3rd
Ⓜ St Paul
Ⓒ 01 42 71 36 70
cafebaci.fr
⊕ 11-12/T11

Café de l'Esplanade
52 r Fabert, 7th
Ⓜ La Tour Maubourg
Ⓒ 01 47 05 38 50
⊕ 10/H11

Café Marly
93 r de Rivoli, 1st
Ⓜ Palais Royal
Ⓒ 01 49 26 06 60
⊕ 6/M9

La Cantine du-Faubourg
105 r du Fbg St-Honoré,
8th
Ⓜ St Philippe du Roule
Ⓒ 01 42 56 22 22
⊕ 1-2/G5

Chez Léa
5 r Claude Bernard, 5th
Ⓜ Censier Daubenton
Ⓒ 01 43 31 46 30
⊕ 15/P17

Chiberta
3 r Arsène-Houssaye, 8th
Ⓜ Charles de Gaulle
Etoile
Ⓒ 01 53 53 42 00
lechiberta.com
⊕ 1-5/E5

Drouant
16 pl Gaillon, 2nd
Ⓜ Quatre Septembre
Ⓒ 01 42 65 15 16
drouant.com
⊕ 6/M7

Fontaine Gaillon
1 pl Gaillon, 2nd
Ⓜ Quatre Septembre
Ⓒ 01 47 42 63 22
la-fontaine-gaillon.fr
⊕ 6/M7

Laurent
41 av Gabriel, 8th
Ⓜ Champs Elysées
Clemenceau
Ⓒ 01 42 25 00 39
le-laurent.com
⊕ 6/I7

Le Pré Verre
8 r Thénard, 5th
Ⓜ Maubert-Mutualité
Ⓒ 01 43 54 59 47
⊕ 11-15/P14

R'aliment
57 r Charlot, 3rd
Ⓜ Temple
Ⓒ 01 48 04 88 28
⊕ 7-8/T9

Relais de Venise
271 bd Pereire Sud, 17th
Ⓜ Porte Maillot
Ⓒ 01 45 74 27 97
⊕ 1/B4

05

Tokyo Eat
Palais du Tokyo,
13 av du Président
Wilson, 16th
Ⓜ Iéna
Ⓒ 01 47 20 00 29
⊕ 5/D9

Ze Kitchen Galerie
4 r des Grands-Augustins,
6th
Ⓜ St Michel
Ⓒ 01 44 32 00 32
zekitchengalerie.fr
⊕ 11/O12

See page 9
to scan the
directory

ENTERTAINMENT
AND NIGHTLIFE

Les Deux Magots
6 place Saint-Germain-des-Prés, 6th

Previous page: Moulin Rouge
82 boulevard de Clichy, 18th

Paris nightlife runs smoothly and elegantly from the apéritif to the dance floor. There is a right time to be everywhere, and picking the moment to arrive is key to a chic night out, and to mingling with the most scintillating crowd. The glamorous Golden Triangle, around the Champs-Elysées, and Saint-Germain-des-Prés, on the Left Bank, are the two most see-and-be-seen spots, with their delectable hotel bars and private clubs, while the Marais offers a very happening bar scene that is uniquely Parisian. Current trends favour sleek decor and a Sex and the City vibe, a transatlantic cross-pollination that shows just how Paris and New York continually influence each other.

06

cafés and people watching

Green and cream lattice chairs, uniformed waiters, and a perfect kir royal… it's a quintessential Parisian scene and this is where you can start your evening with some fabulous people watching. Saint-Germain's **Café de Flore** and **Les Deux Magots** are the sine qua non of café terraces, always buzzing with a mix of well-heeled locals, tourists, fashionistas and the odd celebrity, and maintaining the district's intellectual credentials with a dose of writers and publishers. The smaller **Café de la Mairie** has a deep terrace from which to contemplate the church of Saint-Sulpice, while **La Palette** off the rue de Seine upholds its arty credentials with gallery owners and students from the Ecole des Beaux-Arts among its regulars. **Les Editeurs** on the Carrefour de l'Odéon, a soigné updating of the literary café, is popular with bookish types and intellectual crooners.

In the Marais, wander down the rue Vieille-du-Temple or rue des Archives depending on your orientation. Rue des Archives is filled with pretty boys, congregating at **Les Marronniers** or **Open Café**, especially during the thriving early evening happy hour. The rue Vieille-du-Temple sees a gorgeous young and single crowd move between the **Petit Fer à Cheval**, **Les Philosophes** and hip newcomer **La Perle**, a happening see-and-be-seen drinking spot at night.

A more bohemian café crawl is found on the Canal Saint-Martin, where **Chez Prune** attracts arty locals, who spill out onto the canal banks on summer evenings.

Sassy hotel bars

As in all cosmopolitan cities, a handful of hotel bars have become the most glamorous drinking institutions in town, thanks to top-class mixology and a star-studded crowd. The debonair Colin Peter Field presides over the **Hemingway Bar** at the Ritz, mixing exclusive concoctions for Kate Moss, Naomi Campbell and Bruce Willis. So popular has the tiny, panelled bar become that it has now spilled over to the other side of the corridor, with Colin flitting between the two.

The **Bar du Plaza Athénée**, and the **Bar de l'Hôtel Costes** are both fashion favourites, with very different atmospheres: the first ice-cool, where customers are on display on tall stools up at the bar, and the latter intimately rococo, with plenty of corners where you can hide from the paparazzi.

The **Bar du Murano** also fields a fashion crowd at its contemporary vodka bar. For a leafy terrace, you can't beat the vertical garden of the **Bar du Pershing Hall**, while an arty crowd graces the **Bar de l'Hôtel Amour**. On the rooftop terrace of the **Bar du Raphaël**, you may glimpse a visiting film star but even if not, being high up and outdoors should be enough to satisfy.

06

Cocktail and lounge bars

Less-pricey cocktails and a more laid-back version of the Hemingway Bar can be found at **Le Fumoir**, opposite the Louvre. If you're alone, pose behind a newspaper or with a book from its well-stocked library;

if you're with friends, play backgammon as you sip classic cocktails. Young professionals mingle at **Kong**, located above the Kenzo boutique, which has a fun design with a geisha theme by Philippe Starck.

A kitsch North African pop art theme and booty-shaking rhythms make **Andy Wahloo** the sexiest bar in the Marais. On the Left Bank, a great early-evening spot is **La Mezzanine de l'Alcazar**, with DJs spinning lounge sounds, or **L'Echelle de Jacob**, where well-to-do yuppies meet up before a night on the town.

Pershing Hall
49 rue Pierre Charron, 8th

Near the Golden Triangle, **Le Music-Hall** is an entertaining place to see and be seen, bathed in changing coloured light; newcomer **Queenie** is a very New York-style bar, where the savvy music, superbly mixed cocktails and good-looking crowd may entice you to stay all night.

Late-night bars

Le Rosebud closes at 2am, no later than most bars, but has to be sampled late at night. This Montparnasse whisky and piano bar was a haunt of writer Marguerite Duras, and today attracts a devoted crowd of habitués, including film star Kristen Scott Thomas.

The ultimate late-night spot, **Mathis** is a hotel bar unlike all others. In a seductive setting of kilims and red velvet upholstery, it operates as a private club for actors and French television personalities. If you're lucky, Madame will like the look of you and let you in…

06

Clubs and dancing

With the exception of **Le Showcase**, a fabulous space under the arches of the Pont Alexandre III that combines live rock and nightclubbing, and **Le Paris Paris**, where independent record labels often host soirées for bright young things, most of Paris's hottest nightclubs are private. This doesn't mean you won't get in, but guile must be employed. Plumb any Paris contacts you

Six degrees of titillation

Although Baz Luhrmann's *Moulin Rouge* brought the cancan back into vogue, Paris's saucy side has always been sizzling under the surface. The **Moulin Rouge** may not be the hippest place to be seen, but it still offers a scintillatingly polished show that's not too risqué for trans-Atlantic visitors.

More original is the **Crazy Horse**, a wonderfully kitsch 1970s throwback where almost-nude dancers are "clothed" in revolving light. It has been enjoying a revival thanks to the performances by Ariele Dombasle, the bombshell wife of philosopher Bernard-Henri Lévy. Taking things quite a few steps further, and suddenly very in vogue, **Les Chandelles** is about as hush-hush as you can get. At this exclusive club for swingers or *échangistes*, it is essential to arrive in a couple. Ladies are encouraged to wear their best undergarments – think Alice Cadolle or Fifi Chachnil – and certainly check any inhibitions along with your purse and coat in at the door.

have to get on the guest list, and if that fails arrive before 2am dressed as if on a *Vogue* fashion shoot. (Girls: wear heels, as height seems to be an advantage.)

Top of the club list is **Le Baron**, a former hostess bar where celebs let their hair down on the dance floor. Even smaller (and therefore even more exclusive) is **Black Calvados**, a recent arrival in the Golden Triangle from fashion show producer Alex de Bétak and former Soundgarden frontman Chris Cornell. Models and rock stars cram in to this tiny metal box for private parties; rock chic is the essential dress code.

The extremely select **Le Néo** is John Galliano's home from home with a fashion and pretty boy bias. Meanwhile long-running **L'Etoile** and the **V.I.P. Room**, which has an outpost in Saint-Tropez, are beacons for the glamazon set, and attract visiting celebrities like P. Diddy, Robbie Williams and Pamela Anderson.

06

At **Maxim's** you will find seriously fun club nights, especially the guest-list-only evening held once a month, a favourite with the gay fashion crowd. Finally, **Chez Castel**, hidden away on the Left Bank, is a firm tradition, where aging millionaires and their mistresses, débutantes and call girls down inordinate amounts of Champagne in an atmosphere of louche abandon.

Kong
1 rue du Pont Neuf, 1st

cafés and people watching

Café de Flore
172 bd St-Germain, 6th
Ⓜ St Germain des Prés
Ⓒ 01 45 48 55 26
cafe-de-flore.com
⊕ 10/L12

Les Deux Magots
6 pl St-Germain-des -Prés, 6th
Ⓜ St Germain des Prés
Ⓒ 01 45 48 55 25
lesdeuxmagots.com
⊕ 10/M12

La Palette
43 r de Seine, 6th
Ⓜ Mabillon
Ⓒ 01 43 26 68 15
⊕ 11/N12

Café de la Mairie
8 pl St-Sulpice, 6th
Ⓜ St Sulpice
Ⓒ 01 43 26 67 82
⊕ 10/M13

Les Editeurs
4 carrefour de l'Odéon, 6th
Ⓜ Odéon
Ⓒ 01 43 26 67 76
lesediteurs.fr
⊕ 11/N13

La Perle
78 r Vieille-du-Temple, 4th
Ⓜ St Sébastien Froissart
Ⓒ 01 42 72 69 93
⊕ 11-12/T10

Café des Initiés
3 pl des Deux-Ecus, 1st
Ⓜ Louvre Rivoli
Ⓒ 01 42 33 78 29
⊕ 7/O9

Les Marronniers
18 r des Archives, 4th
Ⓜ Hôtel de Ville
Ⓒ 01 40 27 87 72
⊕ 11/R11

Petit Fer à Cheval
30 r Vieille-du-Temple, 4th
Ⓜ St Paul
Ⓒ 01 42 72 47 47
cafeine.com
⊕ 11/S11

06

Chez Prune
36 r Beaurepaire, 10th
Ⓜ République
Ⓒ 01 42 41 30 47
⊕ 7-8/T7

Open Café
17 r des Archives, 4th
Ⓜ Hôtel de Ville
Ⓒ 01 42 72 26 18
⊕ 11/R11

Les Philosophes
28 r Vieille-du-Temple, 4th
Ⓜ St Paul
Ⓒ 01 48 87 49 64
cafeine.com
⊕ 11/S11

Late-night bars

Chez Carmen
53 r Vivienne, 2nd
Ⓜ Richelieu Drouot
Ⓒ 01 42 36 45 41
⊕ 7/O7

Mathis
3 r de Ponthieu, 8th
Ⓜ Franklin D Roosevelt
Ⓒ 01 53 76 39 55
⊕ 5-6/G6

Le Rosebud
11bis r Delambre, 14th
Ⓜ Vavin
Ⓒ 01 43 35 38 54
⊕ 14/L17

Sassy hotel bars

Bar de l'Hôtel Amour
8 r de Navarin, 9th
Ⓜ St-Georges
Ⓒ 01 48 78 31 80
hotelamour.com
⊕ 3/N3

Bar de l'Hôtel Costes
239 r St-Honoré, 1st
Ⓜ Tuileries
Ⓒ 01 42 44 50 00
hotelcostes.com
⊕ 6/L8

Bar du Murano
13 bd du Temple, 3rd
Ⓜ Filles du Calvaire
Ⓒ 01 42 71 20 00
muranoresort.com
⊕ 8/U8

Bar du Plaza Athénée
25 av Montaigne, 8th
Ⓜ Alma Marceau
Ⓒ 01 53 67 66 00
plaza-athenee-paris.com
⊕ 5/F8

Bar du Pershing Hall
49 r Pierre Charron, 8th
Ⓜ George V
Ⓒ 01 58 36 58 00
pershinghall.com
⊕ 5/F7

Bar du Raphaël
17 av Kléber, 16th
Ⓜ Charles de Gaulle
Etoile
Ⓒ 01 53 64 32 00
raphael-hotel.com
⊕ 5/C7

**Hôtel Trocadéro
Dokhan's Paris**
117 r Lauriston, 16th
Ⓜ Trocadéro
Ⓒ 01 53 65 66 99
dokhans-sofitel-paris.com
⊕ 5/B8

Hemingway Bar
15 pl Vendôme, 1st
Ⓜ Opéra
Ⓒ 01 43 16 45 33
ritzparis.com
⊕ 6/L8

Le Jaipur
Hôtel Vernet,
25 r Vernet, 8th
Ⓜ George V
Ⓒ 01 44 31 98 06
⊕ 5/E6

Six degrees of titillation

Crazy Horse
12 av George V, 8th
Ⓜ Alma Marceau
Ⓒ 01 47 23 32 32
lecrazyhorseparis.com
⊕ 5/E7

Les Chandelles
1 r Thérèse, 1st
Ⓜ Pyramides
Ⓒ 01 42 60 43 31
les-chandelles.com
⊕ 7/N8

Moulin Rouge
82 bd de Clichy, 18th
Ⓜ Blanche
Ⓒ 01 53 09 82 82
moulinrouge.fr
⊕ 2/M2

Cocktail and lounge bars

Andy Wahloo
69 r des Gravilliers, 3rd
Ⓜ Arts et Métiers
Ⓒ 01 42 71 20 38
⊕ 7/R9

Le Bar
27 r de Condé, 6th
Ⓜ Odéon
Ⓒ 01 43 29 06 61
⊕ 11/N13

L'Echelle de Jacob
10-12 r Jacob, 6th
Ⓜ St-Germain-des-Prés
Ⓒ 01 46 34 00 29
echelledejacob.com
⊕ 10/M12

Le Fumoir
6 r de l'Amiral Coligny, 1st
Ⓜ Louvre Rivoli
☎ 01 42 92 00 24
lefumoir.com
⊕ 11/O10

Kong
1 r du Pont Neuf, 1st
Ⓜ Pont Neuf
☎ 01 40 39 09 00
kong.fr
⊕ 11/P10

Clubs and dancing

Black Calvados
40 av Pierre 1er de
Serbie, 8th
Ⓜ George V
☎ 01 47 20 77 77
⊕ 5/E8

Le Baron
6 av Marceau, 8th
Ⓜ Alma Marceau
☎ 01 47 20 04 01
clublebaron.fr
⊕ 5/E8

Chez Castel
15 r Princesse, 6th
Ⓜ Mabillon
☎ 01 40 51 52 80
⊕ 10/M13

Mandalaray
32 r Marbeuf, 8th
Ⓜ Franklin D. Roosevelt
☎ 01 56 88 36 36
mandalaray.com
⊕ 5/F7

**La Mezzanine
de l'Alcazar**
62 r Mazarine, 6th
Ⓜ Odéon
☎ 01 53 10 19 99
alcazar.fr
⊕ 2/M2

L'Etoile
12 r de Presbourg, 16th
Ⓜ Charles de Gaulle
Etoile
☎ 01 45 00 78 70
letoileparis.com
⊕ 1-5/C5

Maxim's
3 r Royale, 8th
Ⓜ Concorde
spiritofstar.com
⊕ 6/K7

Le Néo
23 r de Ponthieu, 8th
Ⓜ Franklin D. Roosevelt
☎ 01 42 25 57 14
⊕ 5-6/G6

Le Music-Hall
63 av Franklin
Roosevelt, 8th
Ⓜ Franklin D. Roosevelt
☎ 01 45 61 03 63
music-hallparis.com
⊕ Off map

Queenie
43 r de Ponthieu, 8th
Ⓜ St Philippe du Roule
☎ 01 42 25 34 04
lequeenie.fr
⊕ 5-6/G6

Le Paris Paris
5 av de l'Opéra, 1st
Ⓜ Palais Royal
leparisparis.com
⊕ 6/M8

06

Le Showcase
Pt Alexandre III, Port de
Chps Elysées, 8th
Ⓜ Chps Elysées Clemenceau
☎ 01 45 61 25 43
showcase.fr
⊕ 6/H9

V.I.P. Room
78 av des Chps Elysées, 8th
Ⓜ George V
☎ 01 56 69 16 66
viproom.fr
⊕ 5/F6

See page 9
to scan the
directory

GRAND HOTELS AND
FASHION FAVOURITES

Hôtel de Crillon
10 place de la Concorde, 8th

Previous page: Hôtel Mayet
3 rue Mayet, 6th

The stylish visitor is spoiled for choice with elegant hotels to suit all tastes. At the top of the ladder are Paris's magnificent palace hotels, some of which inhabit the former *hôtels particuliers*, grand private homes, of wealthy aristocrats; others were purpose built on suitably noble scale during the days of the aristocratic grand tour. Custom from the trans-Atlantic luxury liners brought these hotels to their zenith, and that age of elegance and faultless service is still evoked today. Nowadays, the boutique hotel is à la mode, offering an intimate atmosphere and cutting-edge design but affordable for urbanistas on the move.

07

The ultimate in pampering

How can you choose among Paris's palace hotels when all of them offer the ultimate in luxury: marble bathrooms, exquisite fabrics, and deluxe service? Your selection might be based on the glamorous bars, restaurants and ambience more than on the rooms themselves – bearing in mind that standard rooms may prove more ordinary than you might expect. One place where this is not true is **Le Meurice**, which is looking simply splendid in subtle cream and gold fabrics with original oil paintings on the walls. The prestige doubles on the sixth floor have roll-top baths from which you can gaze at the Eiffel Tower, and tiny balconies overlooking the Tuileries garden.

The **Hôtel de Crillon**, on majestic Place de la Concorde, is a true palace – it was the private residence of the Dukes of Crillon until 1907 – with salons that look like Versailles and a rococo courtyard. Ask for rooms at the front, which retain the original plaster mouldings, and spend time in the Winter Garden looking out for A-listers such as Madonna and Jennifer Lopez.

The legend of the **Ritz** hangs on the many famous people who have stayed, or even lived there, since its inception in 1898. You can book into the former suites of Coco Chanel, Marcel Proust and the Duke and Duchess of Windsor, complete with their own *objets d'art*, a thrilling brush with the past. The hotel also has the ultimate spa, which has a Pompeii-inspired colonnaded swimming pool.

The **Four Seasons Hotel George V Paris** is another A-list favourite packing in more Grammy and Oscar winners per square metre than any other Paris hotel. **Le Bristol** is more discreet and is favoured by visiting dignitaries and foreign royalty.

Paris's newest palace, **Hôtel Fouquet's Barrière**, is firmly aimed at Americans and has larger standard rooms than any other hotel in its class, a huge swimming pool and a traditional decor that incorporates new technology, such as mirrors that become TV screens.

For a truly contemporary palace, follow Sting and Janet Jackson to the **Park Hyatt Paris Vendôme**, designed by the same team as the hotel in *Lost in Translation*. In contrast, the 1920s **Hôtel Raphael** has very traditional rooms and an atmosphere reminiscent of a gentleman's club. Its unique feature, though, is the summer rooftop garden, a true oasis above the Champs-Elysées.

Designer dynamos

A hotel should provide you with your ultimate dream home for a day, so if your idea of style is more Perspex and chrome than chintz and tassels, choose from one of Paris's cutting-edge design hotels. The **Sezz**, in residential Passy near the Pont de Bir Hakeim, which appears in *Last Tango in Paris*, is the most far-out with its grey stone walls, bathrooms behind glass and walkie-talkie-bearing assistants to cater to every whim.

07

In the Golden Triangle, the **Hôtel de Sers** has given a contemporary architectural treatment to a traditional *hôtel particulier* and complements this with modish

Montalembert
3 rue de Montalembert, 7th

custom-designed furniture. It's a favourite with tennis stars playing at the French Open, and its top-floor suites have fabulous terraces that make you feel as though you're in Cannes.

In the Champs-Elysées area, chic minimalist **Hôtel le 'A'** was the first to espouse the gallery hotel concept – as well as artworks in the lobby, each of the 25 rooms boasts its own statement painting by artist Fabrice Hyber. Nearby, **Hôtel Costes K** is like a design gallery, dotted with Pop Art furniture from the private collection of Jean-Louis Costes; its architecture by Ricardo Bofill incorporates an atrium and an underground swimming pool.

Murano Urban Resort, located on the edge of the Marais, sparked the trend for mood lighting you can control yourself, bathing your white room in pink, green or blue auras as you wish. There is also a very of-the-moment bar and fashionista-packed restaurant.

07

The bohemian **Hôtel Amour**, in Pigalle, prides itself on what it has not got (bathrobes, porters, laundry bags, trouser presses). It's the antithesis of a palace hotel, with funky, individual rooms designed by graffiti artist André and his friends and a conscientiously trendy young crowd hanging out at the bar.

Hotels for shopping sprees

If you're looking to shop till you drop, drop in style at the Left Bank's perennially fashionable **Hôtel Montalembert** with its sleek taupe decor. Nearby, the **Esprit Saint-Germain** has a similarly sophisticated vibe with a lovely fireside niche for putting your feet up, while the **Hôtel le Saint-Grégoire** is a warm and intimate boutique hotel.

Grande dame **Hôtel Lutétia** opened in 1910 specifically for shoppers flocking to the Bon Marché department store. Today it's equally appealing for its proximity to the independent shoe stores and fashion boutiques that line nearby rue du Cherche-Midi. Equally convenient is the chic boutique hotel **Le Placide**, whose 11 rooms are brilliantly designed like mini suites.

In the heart of the Right Bank, the **Renaissance Paris Vendôme** is far more sleek than its name suggests, with a Zen influence that runs right down to the food at its Pinxo restaurant. One of Paris's best-kept secrets is its gorgeous slate-walled private swimming pool, which you can often have all to yourself.

Fashionista hotels

Anyone who watches *Sex and the City* will remember the famous scene in the final episode when Carrie

Bradshaw swanned through the **Plaza Athénée** in a sea foam Versace dress. Sarah Jessica Parker may be the face of the Athénée, but the hotel's appeal for fashionistas worldwide has a lot more to do with its location on avenue Montaigne, its gargantuan wardrobe spaces and its proximity to almost every major Parisian couture house.

Fashion editors, designers and models also cluster at **Hôtel Costes**, whose deliciously rococo bar and terrace remain the ultimate see-and-be-seen location. Valentino and Kenzo, however, prefer the understated luxury of the **Hôtel Regina** or the **Pavillon de la Reine**.

Since fashion designes are a famously globe-trotting lot, it's hardly surprising that they have started collaborating on luxury hotels. In Paris, this trend has yielded the playful **Hôtel du Petit Moulin** designed by Christian Lacroix, and Azzedine Alaïa's **3 Rooms**, three exclusive private apartments within his atelier and showroom complex.

Romantic hideaways

The subtle and romantic **Hospes Lancaster,** near the Champs-Elysées, is the home-away-from-home for many American movie stars who adore its discretion. Hide from the paparazzi in the purple-hued Marlene Dietrich suite, or relax in the oasis of the Japanese garden.

Hôtel Duc de Saint-Simon
14 rue de Saint Simon, 7th

From the same owners as Pavillon de la Reine, the **Saint James Paris** is housed in a private club, which feels like a château in the county. Each room in the Terence Conran-designed **La Trémoille**, in the Golden Triangle, offers the option of a seemingly perfectly automised room service, thanks to a hatch between each bedroom and the hallway. Meanwhile, **Pershing Hall** combines elegant hideaway rooms with the chance to meet and mingle in its romantic vertical garden courtyard and mezzanine bar.

In the Marais, the **Hôtel Bourg Tibourg** is a discreet Costes offshoot without the star-studded cast, but with similarly flamboyant Jacques Garcia interiors, here given a neo-Gothic twist.

On the opposite bank lies a wealth of luxurious, romantic charm. The delightful **Relais Christine,** in a gorgeous 16th-century aristocratic mansion, has three suites that each open onto their own private Parisian garden, and alongside its period features has cleverly added a spa in the vaulted cellars. The **Hôtel de l'Abbaye** has welcoming salons, with a log fire in winter, and four duplex suites whose private balconies are lovely for al fresco breakfasts in fine weather. Lauren Bacall's favourite Parisian bolthole is the **Hôtel Duc de Saint-Simon**, arranged around a garden courtyard.

07

The Jacques Garcia-designed **L'Hôtel** has fantasy rooms that evoke the Indian Raj, an 18th-century boudoir or the Orient; the Mistinguett room has the music hall star's original Art Deco bed, while the room where Oscar Wilde stayed is decorated in peacock-feather wallpaper. The Roman-style spa in the cellar is enjoyed in private as only one room can book it at a time.

Budget Chic

Though there may be no shortage of classic and designer hotels in Paris, chic hotels on a shoestring are in short supply. Naturally those that offer the most stylish surroundings and the best value for money get booked up far in advance. Surprisingly, Saint-Germain-des-Prés offers several choices and certainly, smartness is inveterate to this quarter.

The **Clos Médicis** has brought boutique-style minimalist chic to a historic building near the Luxembourg garden. The **Hôtel des Saints-Pères** provides more traditional Parisian elegance. Its rooms offer lofty ceilings and walls hung with old masters. You can almost pretend you are sleeping in your very own private townhouse, especially if you book room 100, the Chambre à la Fresque, with its original 17th-century painted ceiling depicting Leda and the Swan. Nearby and equally full of charm are the **Hôtel Thomas**

d'Aquin with tasteful decor and complimentary Wi-Fi, the **Hôtel le Sainte-Beuve**, decorated by British designer David Hicks, and the discreet **Hôtel Verneuil,** set across the street from the former home of the late Serge Gainsbourg, which is now covered in tributes from his devoted fans.

On the Right Bank, **Hôtel Thérèse** is perfectly placed for visits to the Louvre and the Opéra. The Marais has the **Caron de Beaumarchais**, a lovingly recreated 17th-century time capsule, and the **Hôtel Castex**, both decorated with *toile-de-jouy* fabrics and only minutes from the Place des Vosges,

Modern chic for cool youngsters can be found at the sleek **Hôtel Duo**, spanning two Marais houses near the Centre Pompidou, and industrial chic **Le Général**, likewise designed by Jean-Philippe Nuël, which has a funky bar featuring barmen whose ties match its loud floral wallpaper.

07

Perhaps the hippest budget place of all is the bohemian **Hôtel Eldorado** in the Batignolles quarter near Montmartre. Owned by a former model booker, it is where up-and-coming stars of the catwalk start out before they graduate to grand hotel splendour. Its dreamy garden café is as lovely as any in Paris.

Price indications are for a double room: € up to €100; €€ €101 to €200; €€€ €201 to €350; €€€€ €351 and over.

The ultimate in pampering

Le Bristol €€€€
111 r du Fbg St-Honoré, 8th
Ⓜ Franklin D. Roosevelt
ⓒ 01 53 43 43 00
hotel-bristol.com
⊕ 1-2/G5

Four Seasons Hotel George V Paris €€€€
31 av George V, 8th
Ⓜ George V
ⓒ 01 49 52 70 00
fourseasons.com/paris
⊕ 5/E7

Hôtel de Crillon €€€€
10 pl de la Concorde, 8th
Ⓜ Concorde
ⓒ 01 44 71 15 00
crillon.com
⊕ 6/J8

Hôtel Fouquet's Barrière € €€€
46 av George V, 8th
Ⓜ George V
ⓒ 01 40 69 60 52
fouquets-barriere.com
⊕ 5/E7

Hôtel de Vendôme €€€€
1 pl Vendôme, 1st
Ⓜ Opéra
ⓒ 01 55 04 55 00
hoteldevendome.com
⊕ 6/L8

Hôtel Raphael €€€€
17 av Kléber, 16th
Ⓜ Charles de Gaulle-Etoile
ⓒ 01 53 64 32 00
raphael-hotel.com
⊕ 5/C8

Le Meurice €€€€
228 r de Rivoli, 1st
Ⓜ Tuileries
ⓒ 01 44 58 10 10
meuricehotel.com
⊕ 6/M9

Park Hyatt Paris Vendôme €€€€
5 r de la Paix, 2nd
Ⓜ Opéra
ⓒ 01 58 71 12 34
paris.vendome.hyatt.com
⊕ 6/M7

Le Ritz €€€€
15 pl Vendôme, 1st
Ⓜ Opéra
ⓒ 01 43 16 45 33
ritzparis.com
⊕ 6/L8

Hotels for shopping sprees

Esprit St Germain €€€
22 r St Sulpice, 6th
Ⓜ Mabillon
ⓒ 01 53 10 55 55
espritsaintgermain.com
⊕ 11/N13

Hôtel Lutétia €€€€
46 bd Raspail, 6th
Ⓜ Sèvres Babylone
ⓒ 01 49 54 46 46
lutetia.com
⊕ 10/K13

Hôtel Montalembert €€€€
3 r de Montalembert, 7th
Ⓜ Rue du Bac
ⓒ 01 45 49 68 68
montalembert.com
⊕ 10/L11

Hôtel le St-Grégoire
€€€
43 r de l'Abbé-Grégoire, 6th
Ⓜ St Placide
Ⓒ 01 45 48 23 23
hotelsaintgregoire.com
⊕ 10-14/K14

Le Placide €€€€
6 r St-Placide, 6th
Ⓜ Sèvres Babylone
Ⓒ 01 42 84 34 60
leplacidehotel.com
⊕ 10-14/K14

Renaissance Paris Vendôme €€€€
4 r du Mont Thabor, 1st
Ⓜ Tuileries
Ⓒ 01 40 20 20 00
marriott.com
⊕ 6/K8

Designer dynamos

Hôtel le 'A' €€€€
4 r d'Artois, 8th
Ⓜ St Philippe du Roule
Ⓒ 01 42 56 99 99
paris-hotel-a.com
⊕ 5-6/G6

Hôtel Costes K €€€
81 av Kléber, 16th
Ⓜ Boissière
Ⓒ 01 44 05 75 75
hotelcostesk.com
⊕ 5/C7

Hôtel Sezz €€€
6 av Frémiet, 16th
Ⓜ Passy
Ⓒ 01 56 75 26 26
hotelsezz.com
⊕ Off map

Hôtel Amour €€€
8 r Navarin, 9th
Ⓜ St Georges
Ⓒ 01 48 78 31 80
hotelamour.com
⊕ 3/N3

Hôtel le 123 Elysées
€€€
123 r du Fbg St-Honoré, 8th
Ⓜ St Philippe du Roule
Ⓒ 01 53 89 01 23
astotel.com
⊕ 3/S1

Hôtel le Walt €€€
37 av de la Motte
Picquet, 7th
Ⓜ École Militaire
Ⓒ 01 45 51 55 83
lewaltparis.com
⊕ 9-10/G12

07

Hôtel Bel Ami €€€
7-11 r St Benoît, 6th
Ⓜ St Germain des Prés
Ⓒ 01 42 61 53 53
hotel-bel-ami.com
⊕ 10/M12

Hôtel de Sers €€€€
41 av Pierre 1er de
Serbie, 8th
Ⓜ George V
Ⓒ 01 53 23 75 75
hoteldesers.com
⊕ 5/E8

Murano Urban Resort €€€€
13 bd du Temple, 3rd
Ⓜ Filles du Calvaire
Ⓒ 01 42 71 20 00
muranoresort.com
⊕ 8/U8

Fashionista favourites

3 Rooms €€€€
5 r du Moussy, 4th
Ⓜ Hôtel de Ville
ⓒ 01 44 78 92 00
⊕ 11/R11

Hôtel du Petit Moulin €€
29-31 r de Poitou, 3rd
Ⓜ St Sébastien Froissart
ⓒ 01 42 74 10 10
hoteldupetitmoulin.com
⊕ 11/T10

Pavillon de la Reine €€€€
28 pl des Vosges, 3rd
Ⓜ Chemin Vert
ⓒ 01 40 29 19 19
pavillon-de-la-reine.com
⊕ 12/U12

Hôtel Costes €€€€
239 r St-Honoré, 1st
Ⓜ Tuileries
ⓒ 01 42 44 50 50
hotelcostes.com
⊕ 6/M9

Hôtel Regina €€€€
2 pl des Pyramides, 1st
Ⓜ Tuileries
ⓒ 01 42 60 31 10
regina-hotel.com
⊕ 6/M9

Plaza Athénée €€€€
25 av Montaigne, 8th
Ⓜ Alma Marceau
ⓒ 01 53 67 66 65
plaza-athenee-paris.com
⊕ 5/F8

Romantic hideaways

Hospes Lancaster €€€€
7 r de Berri, 8th
Ⓜ George V
ⓒ 01 40 76 40 76
hotel-lancaster.fr
⊕ 5/F6

Hôtel Duc de Saint-Simon €€€
14 r de St-Simon, 7th
Ⓜ Rue du Bac
ⓒ 01 44 39 20 20
hotelducdesaintsimon.com
⊕ 10/K12

Relais Christine €€€€
3 r Christine, 6th
Ⓜ Odéon
ⓒ 01 40 51 60 80
relais-christine.com
⊕ 11/O12

L'Hôtel €€€€
13 r des Beaux-Arts, 6th
Ⓜ St Germain des Prés
ⓒ 01 44 41 99 00
l-hotel.com
⊕ 11/N12

Hôtel Bourg Tibourg €€€
19 r du Bourg Tibourg, 4th
Ⓜ Hôtel de Ville
ⓒ 01 42 78 47 39
bourgtibourg.com
⊕ 11/R11

Saint James Paris €€€€
43 av Bugeaud, 16th
Ⓜ Porte Dauphine
ⓒ 01 44 05 81 81
saint-james-paris.com
⊕ 5/A7

Hôtel de l'Abbaye €€€
10 r Cassette, 6th
Ⓜ St Sulpice
ⓒ 01 45 44 38 11
hotel-abbaye.com
⊕ 10-14/M14

Pershing Hall €€€€
49 r Pierre Charron, 8th
Ⓜ George V
ⓒ 01 58 36 58 00
pershinghall.com
⊕ 5/F7

La Trémoille €€€€
14 r de La Trémoille, 8th
Ⓜ Alma Marceau
ⓒ 01 56 52 14 00
hotel-tremoille.com
⊕ 5/F8

Budget chic

Caron de Beaumarchais €€
12 r Vieille du Temple, 4th
Ⓜ St Paul
Ⓒ 01 42 72 34 12
carondebeaumarchais.com
⊕ 11/S11

Le Clos Médicis €€
56 r Mr le Prince, 6th
Ⓜ Luxembourg
Ⓒ 01 43 29 10 80
closmedicis.com
⊕ 11-15/O14

Le Général €€
5-7 r Rampon, 11th
Ⓜ Oberkampf
Ⓒ 01 47 00 41 57
legeneralhotel.com
⊕ 8/U8

Hôtel Castex €€
5 r Castex, 4th
Ⓜ Bastille
Ⓒ 01 42 72 31 52
castexhotel.com
⊕ 12/U13

Hôtel Duo €€
11 r du Temple, 4th
Ⓜ Hôtel de Ville
Ⓒ 01 42 72 72 22
duoparis.com
⊕ 11/R10

Hôtel Eldorado €
18 r des Dames, 17th
Ⓜ Place de Clichy
Ⓒ 01 45 22 35 21
eldoradohotel.fr
⊕ 2/K1

Hôtel Mayet €€
3 r Mayet, 6th
Ⓜ Duroc
Ⓒ 01 47 83 21 35
mayet.com
⊕ 14/J15

Hôtel le Sainte-Beuve €€
9 r Ste-Beuve, 6th
Ⓜ Notre D des Champs
Ⓒ 01 45 48 20 07
paris-hotel-charme.com
⊕ 14/L16

Hôtel des Sts-Pères €€
65 r des Sts Pères, 6th
Ⓜ St Germain des Prés
Ⓒ 01 45 44 50 00
paris-hotel-saints-peres.com
⊕ 10/M11

Hôtel Thérèse €€
5-7 r Thérèse, 1st
Ⓜ Pyramides
Ⓒ 01 42 96 10 01
hoteltherese.com
⊕ 7/N8

Hôtel Thomas d'Aquin €€
3 r du Pré aux Clercs, 7th
Ⓜ St Germain des Prés
Ⓒ 01 42 61 01 22
aquin-paris-hotel.com
⊕ 10/L12

07

Hôtel Verneuil €€
8 r de Verneuil, 7th
Ⓜ St-Germain-des-Prés
Ⓒ 01 42 60 82 12
hotelverneuil.com
⊕ 10/l11

See page 9
to scan the
directory

08

SPAS, GROOMING
AND RELAXATION

Autour de Christophe Robin
9 rue Guénégaud, 6th

Previous page: Les Bains du Marais
31 rue des Blancs Manteaux, 4th

The Parisian neighbourhood beauty salon, a kitsch all-pink zone where clients pour out their problems to empathetic beauticians, was brilliantly portrayed in the film *Venus Beauty Institute*, starring Audrey Tautou. However, La Tautou herself is more likely to be found in one of the city's altogether more sybaritic havens. Unsurprisingly, Paris offers a plethora of high-end spas, as well as the individual facial gurus who keep the top French film stars looking gorgeous. Parisiennes have also been quick to adopt the North African tradition of hammams, or Turkish baths, which are often housed in stunningly beautiful tiled surroundings. And since Paris was the place where male grooming first came out of the closet, it also has plenty of places for men to maximize their natural assets.

08

Luxurious spas

Paris's palace hotels all house top class spas offering exclusive treatments in luxurious surroundings, and some are open to non-residents. The **Spa at the Four Seasons Hotel George V** offers some of the most decadent packages in Paris, including the Vision of Beauty, a seven-hour indulgence or, for the more gourmand,

All About Chocolate, which includes a chocolate tasting after your chocolate body scrub, chocolate body wrap and massage. The spa also has a room where couples can enjoy spa treatments together.

Inevitably, Le Meurice also has a wonderfully glamourous and indulgent spa, the **Spa Caudelie**, open only to hotel residents. *Vinothérapie* is the buzz word here, using the powerful antioxidants contained in grape seeds. Hôtel Bel Ami keeps up its sleek contemporary styling in its relaxation centre, **L'Espace Harmonie**. The focus is on massages, including Shiatsu, Tibetan and Ayurvedic massages, and reflexology.

Branded top-class spas with a loyal following include **Le Boudoir d'Annick Goutal**, offering classic treatments inspired by famous French beauties; the very chic **Carita La Maison de Beauté** on the Faubourg Saint Honoré; **Spa Nuxe** with its subtle, plant-based treatments; and the cool, minimalist **eSPAce Payot** day spa, which has a glorious stone-clad swimming pool. The **Villa Thalgo** offers thalassotherapy treatments without having to leave for the coast. With parlours in various locations across Paris, **Institut Sara** also provides a range of top-notch treatments, from facials to anti-cellulite body sculpting, as well as useful basics like waxing and manicures.

Eastern influences

An holistic oriental approach has inspired many of the newest spas, which propose a plethora of massages as a complement to aesthetic treatments. Stéphane Jaulin, a former beauty buyer at Colette, opened **Appartment 217** to promote a holistic and biological approach to beauty in a setting designed according to Feng Shui principles. One of the most popular treatments is the Japanese Lyashi Dome, slimming and detoxing your body with a gentle steam.

At the fun and funky **La Bulle Kenzo**, two giant *bulles* or balls dominate the space. One sparkling massage *bulle*, complete with shimmering surfaces and a disco ball, the other, a cocoon massage *bulle*. All treatments are based on tactile experiences for your entire body, encompassing the senses of vision and hearing as well that of touch. At l'**Institut des Cinq Mondes**, you can globe trot from your massage couch with beauty rituals that come from as far afield as Japan, Thailand and Morocco.

Hammams and steam rooms

An authentic North African steam bath is found at the **Hammam de la Mosquée de Paris**. Originally built for the Muslim community, this stunning tiled and domed hammam has become a chic weekend ritual for

08

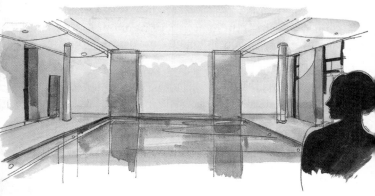

Espace Payot
62 rue Pierre Charron, 8th

svelte Parisiennes, who, contrary to the North African practice of nude bathing, sport their best Princesse Tamtam bikinis in the baths.

Luxury versions of the hammam are found at **La Sultane de Saba** and **Les Bains du Marais**, where couples can steam together (swimming costume obligatory) at weekends and on Wednesday nights.

Star facials

Red-carpet stars, icons and fresh-faced beauties, such as Vanessa Paradis, all keep their skin in tip-top condition with specialist treatments. **Joëlle Ciocco**, who has worked with many a famous face, is a biochemist by training. She will diagnose your skin type and adapt a treatment to correct your skin's imperfections. It is Joëlle's products that are used by the UK's Dr Jean-Louis Sebagh, Madonna's famous dermatologist, in his private practice.

Odile Lecoin is known for her crystal treatments, creating four solutions that can be adapted for all skin types. Another celebrated skin guru is **Gisèle Delorme**, a beautician who creates bespoke treatments using the most luxurious, pure essential oils. Catherine Deneuve and many other French stars favour **Institut Françoise Morice** for its facial treatments and massages.

08

Heavenly hairdressing

If you do nothing else beauty-wise in Paris, enjoy a *brushing* (blow dry) with one of its top stylists. Whatever you are wearing, a soigné hairdo will make all the difference as to how you are treated as you shop and meet people. Perfect for those who wish to remain incognito, superstar hair stylist Jean-Claude Gallon has created a safe haven for the harassed celebrity looking for a discreet update at his salon **Cheveux by Jean-Claude Gallon** where personal, private styling cabins can be provided.

If you are looking for a high level of pampering in addition to expert hair care, book a day at **Alexandre Zouari**, a stylist who is known as the *chou-chou*, or darling, of Parisian society ladies. Zouari has recently joined forces with Pangkor Laut and Tanjong Jara, two luxury retreats in Malaysia, and has transplanted three of their best talents to Paris in an effort to recreate sublime traditional Asian treatments.

Alexandre de Paris, situated on prestigious avenue Matignon, is another society favourite with a loyal following of *grandes dames*. He is just the kind of person who might have had a hand in the transformation of a Leslie Caron-esque Gigi. Every generation from *grand-mère* to *bébé* comes to this institution.

Kylie Minogue and a gaggle of French celebrities are fans of famed hair colourist Christophe Robin, also a consultant to L'Oréal, who has assembled a talent-heavy group of friends in a 17th-century *hôtel particulier* in Saint-Germain at **Autour de Christophe Robin**. Joëlle Ciocco, osteopath Grégor Schultze, make-up artist Mina Matsumura, and Bastien Gonzalez, the fingernail guru who is often flown around the world for his expertise, are all available at the location and hence appointments should be made well in advance. A more analytical approach to hair, similar to that of the skincare gurus, is provided by **Leonor Greyl**, whose personal diagnosis should find the remedy to all your hair care problems.

Just for men

When Philippe Dumont opened **Nickel** in 1996, the world's first spa for men caused a revolution. Nickel has now opened branches in London, New York and San Francisco, proving that men need facials, manicures and pedicures just as much as women if they're going to feel and look *nickel* (clean and impeccable). It has since been joined by **Booster**, whose 20-minute express facial is an ideal pick-me-up before in interview or a date. Meanwhile, the **Institut Marc Delacre** offers facials, manicures, massages and tanning in addition to hairdressing in a traditional masculine atmosphere.

08

Alain Maître Barbier
8 rue Saint Claude, 3rd

New men are also flocking to **Skeen,** a phenomenal men's skincare shop that has also launched cosmetics. Don't be afraid to ask for instructions or advice, the staff love to help and will make the experience comfortable and informative.

For a return to gentlemanly values of old, **Alain, Maître Barbier** upholds a time-honoured practice, offering an authentic barbershop experience using a blade and other traditional tools. Alain is a true specialist of the *barbe*, so your facial hair will look as smart as can be.

Chic workouts

A long day of shopping is not the only kind of exercise to partake in, so for something more energetic consider booking time at the **Ritz Health Club**, a glorious space with Pompeian murals, swimming pool, steam and sauna, and top-of-the-range equipment with personal trainers on hand.

L'Usine, a stylish three-level space near Opéra, is where the health-conscious fashion crowd goes. You can make flexible bookings, taking advantage of its machines, wide choice of classes, on-site instructors and a relaxation spa. West Gomez is another well-known personality in health circles; at his **Etre Bien,**

08

Tout Simplement studios the coaching is top notch. Alongside traditional gym classes it offers pilates and power plate.

Bikram yoga fans need not panic, **Yoga Bikram Paris** runs 71 classes per week, some in English. For Iyengar yoga, **Studio Anjaliom** has one of the most attractive spaces in the city, and Maryam Askari makes her classes bilingual when English speakers are present. Angelina Jolie has been known to put in an appearance here, taking Maddox to its children's yoga class.

Make-up and make-overs

Once your day of pampering or workout is over, a quick make-up revamp will ready you for a night on the town. Bring your cosmetic bag into **By Terry** for expert advice on which products work for you and how to get the best results. The consultation finishes with a full application. **La Boutique Lancôme**, **Guerlain**, and **Les Salons du Palais-Royal Shiseido** are other well-known beauty and make-up destinations.

Luxurious spas

Le Boudoir d'Annick Goutal
14 r Castiglione, 1st
Ⓜ Tuileries
Ⓒ 01 42 60 52 82
annick-goutal.com
⊕ 6/L8

Carita La Maison de Beauté
11 r du Fbg St-Honoré, 8th
Ⓜ Concorde
Ⓒ 01 44 94 11 11
maisondebeautecarita.com
⊕ 6/J7

L'Espace Harmonie
7 r St Benoît, 6th
Ⓜ St-Germain-des-Prés
Ⓒ 01 42 61 53 53
hotel-bel-ami.fr
⊕ 10/M12

Espace Payot
62 r Pierre Charron, 8th
Ⓜ Franklin D. Roosevelt
Ⓒ 01 45 61 42 08
espacepayot.com
⊕ 5/F7

Institut Sara
125 r de la Pompe, 16th
Ⓜ Victor Hugo
Ⓒ 01 47 27 44 72
institutsara.fr
⊕ 5/A7

Spa at the Four Seasons Hotel George V
31 av George V, 8th
Ⓜ George V
Ⓒ 01 49 52 70 00
fourseasons.com/paris
⊕ 5/E7

Spa Caudelie
Le Meurice,
228 r de Rivoli, 1st
Ⓜ Tuileries
Ⓒ 01 44 58 10 10
lemeurice.fr
⊕ 6/K8

Spa Nuxe
32 r Montorgueil, 1st
Ⓜ Etienne-Marcel
Ⓒ 01 55 80 71 40
nuxe.com
⊕ 7/P8

La Villa Thalgo
218 r du Fbg St-Honoré, 8th
Ⓜ George V
Ⓒ 01 45 62 00 20
villathalgo.fr
⊕ 1-5/F5

08

Hammams and steam rooms

Les Bains du Marais
31 r des Blancs Manteaux, 4th
Ⓜ Rambuteau
Ⓒ 01 44 61 02 02
lesbainsdumarais.com
⊕ 11/S11

Hammam de la Mosquée de Paris
39 r Geoffroy St Hilaire, 5th
Ⓜ Censier Daubenton
Ⓒ 01 43 31 38 20
la-mosquee.com
⊕ 15/R17

La Sultane de Saba
8bis r Bachaumont, 2nd
Ⓜ Sentier
Ⓒ 01 40 41 90 95
lasultanedesaba.com
⊕ 7/P8

Star facials

Espace Beauté Chanel Précision
Galeries Lafayette, 40 bd Haussmann, 9th
Ⓜ Havre Caumartin
Ⓒ 01 42 81 06 44
⊕ 2-6/K5

Institut Françoise Morice
58bis r François 1er, 8th
Ⓜ George V
Ⓒ 01 42 56 14 08
francoise-morice.fr
⊕ 5/F7

Joëlle Ciocco
8 pl de la Madeleine, 8th
Ⓜ Madeleine
Ⓒ 01 42 60 58 80
joelle-ciocco.com
⊕ 6/K7

Gisèle Delorme
4 r du Bouloi, 1st
Ⓜ Louvre Rivoli
Ⓒ 01 42 33 23 22
gisele-delorme.com
⊕ 7/O9

Institut Sothys
128 r du Fbg St-Honoré, 8th
Ⓜ George V
Ⓒ 01 53 93 91 53
sothys.com
⊕ 1-5/F5

Odile Lecoin
75 av Paul Doumer, 16th
Ⓜ La Muette
Ⓒ 01 45 04 91 85
odilelecoin.com
⊕ 9/A10

Heavenly hairdressing

Alexandre de Paris
3 av Matignon, 8th
Ⓜ Franklin D. Roosevelt
Ⓒ 01 42 25 57 90
michel-dervyn.com/
alexandre
⊕ 6/H7

Autour de Christophe Robin
(by appointment)
9 r Guénégaud, 6th
Ⓜ Mabillon
Ⓒ 01 42 60 99 15
colorist.net
⊕ 11/N12

Institut Jacques Dessange
6 av de la République, 11th
Ⓜ République
Ⓒ 01 43 57 07 49
⊕ 8/U8

Alexandre Zouari
1 av du Président
Wilson, 8th
Ⓜ Alma Marceau
Ⓒ 01 47 23 79 00
alexandre-zouari.com
✣ 7/O9

Cheveux by Jean-Claude Gallon
3 r Paul-Louis Courier, 7th
Ⓜ Rue du Bac
Ⓒ 01 42 22 04 36
jc-gallon-cheveux.com
✣ 10/K12

Léonor Greyl
15 r Tronchet, 8th
Ⓜ Madeleine
Ⓒ 01 42 65 32 26
leonorgreyl.com
✣ 6/K6

Just for men

Alain Maître Barbier
(by appointment)
8 r St Claude, 3rd
Ⓜ St Sébastien Froissart
Ⓒ 01 42 77 55 80
maitrebarbier.com
✣ 12/U10

Booster
34 r de Provence, 9th
Ⓜ Le Peletier
Ⓒ 01 53 20 04 84
institutbooster.com
✣ 3-7/O5

Nickel
48 r des Francs Bourgeois,
3rd
Ⓜ St Paul
Ⓒ 01 42 77 41 10
nickel.fr
✣ 11-12/T11

Alexander's
15 av de la Motte
Picquet, 7th
Ⓜ la Motte-Picquet
Grenelle
Ⓒ 01 47 05 80 79
✣ 9-13/E14

Institut Marc Delacre
17 av George V, 8th
Ⓜ George V
Ⓒ 01 40 70 99 70
marcdelacre.com
✣ 5/E7

Skeen
21 r des Archives, 4th
Ⓜ Hôtel de Ville
Ⓒ 01 42 76 04 07
skeen.fr
✣ 11/R11

08

Eastern influences

Appartement 217
217 r St-Honoré, 1st
Ⓜ Tuileries
Ⓒ 01 42 96 00 96
lappartement217.com
✣ 6/M8

La Bulle Kenzo
1 r du Pont Neuf, 1st
Ⓜ Pont Neuf
Ⓒ 01 73 04 20 04
labullekenzo.com
✣ 11/P10

L'Institut des Cinq Mondes
6 sq de l'Opéra Louis
Jouvet, 9th
Ⓜ Opéra
Ⓒ 01 42 66 00 60
cinqmondes.com
✣ 6/L6

L'Usine
8 rue de La Michodière, 2nd

Chic workouts

Etre Bien,
Tout Simplement
57 bd de Montmorency,
16th
Ⓜ Porte d'Auteuil
Ⓒ 01 53 92 08 08
westgomez.com
⊕ Off map

Le Studio Pilates
(by appointment)
39 r du Temple, 4th
Ⓜ Hôtel de Ville
Ⓒ 01 42 72 91 74
⊕ 11/R10

L'Usine
8 r de La Michodière, 2nd
Ⓜ Quatre Septembre
Ⓒ 01 42 66 30 30
usineopera.com
⊕ 6/M6

Studio Anjaliom
144 bd de la Villette, 19th
Ⓜ Colonel Fabien
Ⓒ 01 42 00 54 20
anjaliom.com
⊕ 4/V3

Ritz Health Club
15 pl Vendôme, 1st
Ⓜ Opéra
Ⓒ 01 43 16 30 60
ritzparis.com
⊕ 6/L8

Yoga Bikram Paris
13 r Simon Le Franc, 4th
Ⓜ Rambuteau
Ⓒ 01 42 47 18 52
bikramyogaparis.com
⊕ 11/R10

Make-up and make-overs

La Boutique Lancôme
29 r du Fbg St-Honoré,
8th
Ⓜ Concorde
Ⓒ 01 42 65 30 74
lancome.fr
⊕ 6/J7

Guerlain
68 av des Champs
Elysées, 8th
Ⓜ Franklin D. Roosevelt
Ⓒ 01 45 62 52 57
guerlain.com
⊕ 6/H7

MAC
324 r St-Honoré, 1st
Ⓜ Tuileries
Ⓒ 01 42 44 28 91
⊕ 6/M8

08

By Terry
21 passage Véro-Dodat, 1st
Ⓜ Palais Royal
Ⓒ 01 44 76 00 76
byterry.com
⊕ 7/O9

Jeany Rahmé
*(by appointment, home
visits)*
Ⓒ 06 11 59 71 08

**Les Salons du Palais
Royal Shiseido**
142 galerie de Valois, 1st
Ⓜ Palais Royal
Ⓒ 01 49 27 09 09
salons-shiseido.com
⊕ 7/N9

See page 9
to scan the
directory

09

PROPERTY HOT SPOTS
FOR FINE LIVING

Place de Furstenberg, 6th

Previous page: Ile de la Cité

Whether you want to buy or rent, the Internet is a useful tool for gaining an overview of what is on the market. The leading newspaper for property is *Le Figaro*, which publishes property advertisements every Tuesday and Thursday.

The different *quartiers* of Paris each have their distinct character, price bracket and architectural style. Once you've decided you want to live in Paris, start by narrowing down your choice of district and then target selected agencies in the area, giving precise details of your criteria so as to be top of the list when a desirable property comes in. Be prepared to be placed on a waiting list for months. And if a *hôtel particulier* is what you are interested in, be ready to spend a cool €5 million – if you are lucky enough to come across one that is for sale.

If you are only planning on a short stay, furnished apartment rentals can be the answer. Whereas unfurnished flats are generally let on three-year leases, furnished apartments are let on short leases of between one week and one year.

09

The chic Rive Gauche

South of the Seine, the most desirable parts of the *Rive Gauche* (Left Bank) lie in the 5th, 6th and 7th *arrondissements*, plus bordering parts of the 13th and 14th.

Saint-Germain-des-Prés is the most sought-after district in Paris: architecturally beautiful and inveterately chic, with everything you might want on your doorstep or wittin walking distance. Its main downfall is the shortage of parking places. Be prepared to visit apartments in old buildings without a lift – preservation orders mean that it is sometimes impossible to fit one and this is the price you may have to pay for Saint-Germain's old world charm. Most visitors looking for a pied-à-terre head for the area between boulevard Saint-Germain and the Seine. The southern 6th *arrondissement* area of Notre-Dame-des-Champs, near the Jardin du Luxembourg, is calmer.

For a more peaceful, yet still lively neighbourhood, choose the streets around Bon Marché, such as rue du Cherche-Midi. Northwest of Bon Marché in the 7th *arrondissement* is the "embassy quarter". Rue Las Cases or rue Barbet de Jouy are two of the most expensive streets in Paris. Despite its fine 18th-century buildings, it has the reputation of being a "dead" area, especially in the evenings when the streets often seem deserted.

A livelier enclave lies in the area around rue Cler and rue Saint-Dominique known as Le Gros Caillou.

The Latin Quarter

The Latin Quarter in the 5th *arrondissement* east of boulevard Saint-Michel retains a more intellectual aura, as befits its numerous university faculties and research institutes, and is a favourite with writers and academics. Properties range from medieval tenements to 19th-century Haussmannian architecture. The most sought-after district borders rue Soufflot and the Jardins du Luxembourg, where being able to jog, play tennis or simply wander in the gardens is certainly "living the dream" for many who move here.

The Greater Rive Gauche

Southeast of the Latin Quarter, La Butte aux Cailles is a charming village-like enclave amid the vast swathes of modern buildings in the 13th *arrondissement*, from the 1970s tower blocks of Chinatown to the Paris Rive Gauche development zone around the Bibliothèque Nationale François Mitterrand.

09

Head to Montparnasse and you will feel as though you are about to enter the Paris of the 1920s. Montparnasse has kept its artistic feel and its famous brasseries attract a mix of local eccentrics and celebrities. Those

La Tour Montparnasse, 15th

in the know seek out the artists's studios that hide in backstreets or in courtyards, especially around the rue Daguerre market street in the 14th *arrondissement*. Near here, the former *atelier* of artist Tamara de Lempicka went for €2.7 million in 2007 and the house of actor André Dussolier on rue Cels sold for €2.5 million. Nearby Alésia is also known for its village atmosphere. Little houses occasionally come up for sale but don't expect anything for under €2.5 million. Towards Parc Montsouris is another spot with secret passageways, such as Villa Seurat where Henry Miller and Anaïs Nin lived.

Smart western Paris

Further west, the 15th *arrondissement* is a notoriously quiet neighbourhood with a very traditional French lifestyle; the two most interesting areas are square Georges Brassens, near Porte de Versailles, and around rue du Commerce.

Across the Seine on the *Rive Droite* (Right Bank), the 16th *arrondissement* is still very much poodles and pearls territory, though it benefits from some extremely fine 19th-century and early 20th-century architecture and proximity to the Bois de Boulogne. In the southern half, sleepy Auteuil feels like a rural though exceedingly chic village. Any street around rue de Passy, rue de la Pompe and rue de Longchamp or toward Place Victor Hugo will remain a good investment and the 16th on the whole has a stable and good market value. If you are in the market for an *hôtel particulier*, the 16th is a good source with several discreet crescents of private houses.

A new trend here is the "palace apartment building." For their first joint-venture outside the UK, Conran & Partners and City Loft Developments transformed 81 avenue Victor Hugo, a 19th-century townhouse once home to the Romanian Princess Bassaraba de Brancoran, into 34 North American condo-style service apartments.

09

The two neighbourhoods to consider in the 17th are around rue Poncelet and between Parc Monceau and rue Levis. In the 8th, even though the "Golden Triangle" is known for its nightlife and high-end shopping, it is not the most practical area to live in because of its lack of everyday shops and services.

The Marais

Within seconds of seeing Place des Vosges and any adjoining street, you will want to live there. The Marais can be maddening as visitors fill up the narrow streets quickly, especially at weekends, as this is one of the rare parts of Paris where stores open on Sunday. However, the Marais appeals to many as it offers the experience of living in a historic beamed building. Its beautiful architecture, central location, thriving gay scene, original fashion boutiques and the cluster of Jewish delis on rue des Rosiers make the Marais a gem. On the downside, its popularity can make it seem full to bursting, which can make the equally pretty but calmer Saint-Paul district south of rue Saint-Antoine an appealing alternative.

Montorgueil and Palais Royal

An area that has been undergoing rapid transformation is the Montorgueil quartier, centred on an old market street north of Les Halles. It feels rather like London's Covent Garden due to its proximity to theatres, shopping and nightlife areas and it's quiet, traffic-free nature. A little further north is the traditional textile and tailoring district of Sentier, which is where the best value for money will be found.

Palais Royal is another elegant area and if you can't help but live as close as possible to Place Vendôme then rue Saint-Honoré and rue du Mont Thabor between here and the place du Marché Saint-Honoré are the streets to target.

Pigalle and Montmartre

With its early Haussmannian architecture and the wonderful food shops of rue des Martyrs, south Pigalle – now dubbed SoPi – in the 9th *arrondissement* is rising in popularity. Many streets are quite traffic laden, so pick your apartment carefully: courtyard views can be an advantage here in order to avoid the roar of early-morning moped riders. Hilly Montmartre offers the full gamut, from houses with gardens fetching millions on avenue Junot, to rather insalubrious areas with the lowest property prices in Paris. Bear in mind you will be walking up those hundreds of steps with your luggage and shopping, which is fine for a week's Parisian idyll, but maybe not so practical for real life.

09

Bibliothèque Nationale Française
Site François Mitterand
Quai françois Mauriac, 13th

Village des Batignolles

Another burgeoning area is the Batignolles, west of
Montmartre. It may seem a little removed, but that's
one reason it still has deals. At the eastern edge is the
mildly gamy Place de Clichy, to the north the Square
des Batignolles. Hidden throughout are quiet streets,
green spaces and bargains. Think of it as the French
equivalent of Murray Hill, but with more places to
pause: the Square des Batignolles, for its benches, and
bakeries like Laurent Connan (38, rue des Batignolles)
and Franck Perotti (11, rue Flaubert).

The east side

The Faubourg Saint-Denis is a colourful multi-
ethnic area boasting some fine apartment buildings. The Canal Saint Martin with its romantic

metal bridges and lively cafés is more bobo, while across the canal towards Belleville, place Sainte-Marthe is another burgeoning property hotpot.

Oberkampf is a great location for young aspiring artists, with a busy bar scene at night. East of Bastille, the old furniture-makers quarter of Faubourg Saint-Antoine attracts architects and filmmakers, particularly around Marché d'Aligre and passages off rue de Charonne. Further south, the modern apartments around Parc de Bercy are a favourite with families.

Bercy Village

The lower East Side offers properties with contemporary architecture. Bercy Village is a big favourite with families. Across the Seine, linked to Bercy Village by the Simone de Beauvoir bridge, the new area christined "Paris Rive Gauche" even though it is not Rive gauche is built around the Bibliothèque Nationale de France (National Library).

09

Exclusive estate agents

Emile Garcin, an estate agency specialised in high-end sales and rentals, and **Daniel Féau** are experts in guiding their international clientele through the trappings of buying property in France. **Ateliers, Lofts & Associés** is an agency that concentrates on lofts and studio conversions. **Terrasses et Jardins** is the place to go if you want to sunbathe on a rooftop garden, while **Paris 1930** specialises in 1930s Art Deco properties.

House hunters and relocation agents

Finding a suitable property requires enormous legwork. By using a search agency, such as **Home Safari**, you only go to one company, which then does everything for you. Along with their network in real estate, such agencies guide you smoothly through the purchase process, putting you in touch with legal, financial and insurance advisors, designers, tradespeople and architects. **Paris Property Finders** specialises in searching and finding the perfect property in and around Paris. Catherine and Chantal at **Dream Home in Paris** call themselves "property assistants" and are dedicated to providing turnkey solutions for your dream home.

Website homeforswap.com has a novel solution to house hunting: simply exchange your home with that of someone else in another part of the world.

Interior design and renovation

Once you have selected your dream home, you need to find the right interior designer to bring it to fruition. **Sarah Lavoine**, who specialises in interior architecture and decoration, has a casually elegant style.

For those with grandiose tastes, Jean Pablo Molyneux, at **JP Molyneux Studio**, is an impeccably stylish Chilean and long-standing favourite of *Architectural Digest*, who has been decorating elegant homes across the globe for the past 20 years.

Newer kids on the block, **Coorengel & Calvagrac** call themselves "architectural poets, sensory innovators and interior engineers." With an intriguing mix of forward thinking and historic influences, they will transform your property into a unique, statement-making environment.

If you're looking for the readymade article, then Alon and Betsy Kasha are two New York (via London) transplants who create stunning turnkey properties for their company **A + B Kasha**. Passionate about authenticity and design, the Kashas source apartments in the Left Bank with high potential, transforming outmoded dwellings into the ultimate in elegant, modern sophistication. Using local craftsmen, the finest materials and savoir-faire cultivated in their previous careers in luxury goods and finance, the end product is an effortlessly luxurious collaboration; and even comes with a two-year guarantee.

09

Exclusive estate agents

Ateliers, Lofts & Associés
Ⓒ 01 53 00 99 00
ateliers-lofts.com

Daniel Féau
140 r du Fbg St-Honoré, 1st
Ⓜ St-Philippe-du-Roule
Ⓒ 01 53 53 07 07
feau-immobilier.fr
⊕ 1-2/G5

District Immobilier
31 r des Deux Ponts
Ⓜ St Paul
Ⓒ 01 40 62 77 80
district-immo.com
⊕ 11/S13

Emile Garçin
5 r de l'Université, 7th
Ⓜ St-Germain-des-Prés
Ⓒ 01 42 61 73 38
emilegarcin.fr
⊕ 10/L11

Immobilier Ile St Louis
62 r St-Louis-en-l'Ile
Ⓜ Pont Marie
Ⓒ 01 43 26 22 63
11/S13

John Taylor
62 r St Didier, 16th
Ⓜ Victor Hugo
Ⓒ 01 47 27 10 10
john-taylor.fr
⊕ 5/A8

Paris 1930
Ⓒ 01 44 40 48 57
paris1930.com

Le Village Des Batignoles
68 pl du Docteur Felix
Lobligeois, 17th
Ⓒ 01 40 25 99 19
Ⓜ Rome
le-village-des-batignoles.fr
⊕ 2/J2

Terrasses et Jardins
Ⓒ 01 47 27 10 50
terrasses-jardins.com

House hunters and relocation agents

Cosmopolitan Services
64 bd Malesherbes, 8th
Ⓜ Villiers
Ⓒ 01 44 90 10 12
cosmopolitanservices.com
⊕ 2/H3

Dream Home in Paris
15 r du Conseiller
Collignan, 16th
Ⓜ La Muette
Ⓒ 01 46 47 90 25
dreamhomeinparis.com
⊕ 7/N7

**France Global
Relocation**
5 r Mayran, 9th
Ⓜ Cadet
Ⓒ 01 53 20 01 01
fgrelocation.com
⊕ 3/P4

Home Safari
Ⓒ 01 46 03 90 16
home-safari.com

Paris Property Finders
Ⓒ 01 72 77 00 39
parispropertyfinders.com

Paris Relocation Service
30 r Godot de Mauroy, 9th
Ⓜ Madeleine
Ⓒ 01 53 30 41 52
prs.fr
⊕ 6/L6

Rentals and serviced apartments

A la Carte Paris
ⓒ 01 42 46 42 57
alacarte-paris-
apartments.com

Frenchy rentals
ⓒ 01 48 74 66 09
frenchyrentals.com

Interior Immobilier
ⓒ 06 25 90 44 16
interior-immobilier.com

At Home in Paris
ⓒ 01 42 12 40 40
athomeinparis.com

**Guest Apartment
Services**
ⓒ 01 44 07 06 20
guestapartment.com

Parisian Home
ⓒ 01 45 08 03 37
parisianhome.com

Property websites for rentals and sales

seloger.com

explorimmo.com

pap.fr

Interior design and renovation

A + B Kasha
52 r de l'Université, 7th
Ⓜ Rue du Bac
ⓒ 01 45 44 08 10
abkasha.com
✧ 10/L11

**Décoration Jacques
Garcia**
212 r de Rivoli, 1st
Ⓜ Tuileries
ⓒ 01 42 97 48 70
✧ 6/L9

Sarah Lavoine
43 r Saint-Augustin, 2nd
Ⓜ Opéra
ⓒ 01 42 96 34 35
sarahlavoine.com
✧ 7/N7

**Atelier François
Catroux**
20 r Fbg St-Honoré, 8th
Ⓜ Madeleine
ⓒ 01 42 66 69 25
✧ 6/5G

Frédéric Mechiche
4 r Thorigny, 3rd
Ⓜ St Paul
ⓒ 01 42 78 78 28
✧ 11-12/t10

Solution
12 r Dupetit Thouars, 3rd
Ⓜ Temple
ⓒ 01 42 77 27 72
solution-co.com
✧ 7-8/T8

Coorengel & Calvagrac
43 r de l'Echiquier, 10th
Ⓜ Bonne Nouvelle
ⓒ 01 40 27 14 65
coorengel-calvagrac.com
✧ 7/Q6

JP Molyneux Studio
4 r Chapon, 3rd
Ⓜ Arts et Métiers
ⓒ 01 49 96 63 30
✧ 7/R9

Spacio Creative Living
92 r de Rivoli, 4th
Ⓜ St Paul
ⓒ 08 72 84 71 37
spacio.fr
✧ 11/S12

09

See page 9
to scan the
directory

ELITE LIFESTYLE
SERVICES

Colin Peter Field, head barman of the Hemingway Bar

Previous page: Ritz Hemingway Bar

G etting behind the scenes and under the skin of the city is all very well, but what about when you just need a plain old helicopter or personal shopper to guide you through the *mêlée*? Luckily, there are services aplenty, from private guided tours to personal shoppers via concierges who'll arrange tickets to sold out events.

Arriving in style

When chauffeur services are called for, **Executive Travel Services** will transport you smoothly in its fleet of luxury automobiles with bilingual drivers. For wheels with style, **Luxury & Services Rent a Car** has a fleet of sporty Aston Martins, Porsches, Ferraris and Maseratis to hire, or can provide a prestige car with a chauffeur. For a quick getaway, **HéliFrance** can just drop you off at the nearest airfield, where your private jet awaits, of course. It also arranges aerial tours over Paris, giving a truly spectacular view of the city.

10

Tailor-made tours

An entrée into insider Paris, **Pamela H. Darling** can open doors to places and experiences not on the usual tourist beat. She specialises in creating tailored prestige cultural events for individuals and small groups, which have included private tours and receptions at the Musée and Atelier Cartier, the apartments of Mademoiselle Chanel and the magnificent private salons at Christofle. Having married into a family of Franco-American art enthusiasts and collectors, her access to private archives and museums is unheard of, and she boasts a *carnet* of addresses second to none.

Art enthusiasts will also love **Paris Muse**, which promises to make your museum visit "the contemplative experience art was intended to provide." Set up by American art historian Ellen McBreen, Muse has a bank of art experts, including PhD candidates, able to provide a fascinating and interactive look at the city's great art treasuree.

Alice Off Course also offers genuine insider know-how with her tours à la carte. Focusing on culture, cuisine or shopping in any shape or form you desire, the tours are private and groups can be a maximum of four. Alice, an ex-model, is glamorous to the core but also incredibly knowledgeable and makes a pleasant Parisian companion for the day.

Food writer Rosa Jackson of **Edible Paris** can develop a written foodie itinerary just for you with personal introductions to gourmet producers. She can also take the hassle out of arranging your restaurant bookings.

For a splendidly nostalgic tour of the French capital, a fun choice is **4 roues sous 1 parapluie**, who speed you round the city in a vintage convertible Citroën 2CV, attracting admiring stares from fans of this iconic French car. If you prefer getting up some speed, moto-taxi firm **Hégé Service** can take you on a lightening tour on the back of a Honda Goldwing, with commentary by knowledgeable drivers through the two-way microphone. This is a fabulous way to see the futuristic landscape of La Défense by night.

Personal shopping

No time to scour the boutiques of the Marais for your Parisian wardrobe? In partnership with Bon Marché, **Vendôme Services** can offer you a relaxed personal shopping experience with its talented stylists, and can also reserve private showings of creations by Valentino, Alaïa, Alexander McQueen and top jewellery designers in the Plaza Athénée.

10

For a complete image transformation, try **La Mode, Le Club**, which will pick you up from your hotel and take you through hair styling, make-up and personal shopping, finishing with a glass of Champagne.

Personal shopper **Eugénie de Rougé** can transform your look from drab to fab, taking into account a range of budgets. Find the perfume that's perfect for you with a session with a "nose" at the **Atelier de Parfum Guerlain**. Both adults and children can leave with their own bottled concoction.

Concierge services

If you are staying in Paris for a while, make life easy for yourself by hiring a concierge service. **Wecandoo**, **My Hôtel Particulier** and **Quintessentially** will act as your personal Jeeves, arranging anything from dry-cleaning to dog walking, opera tickets to private gallery viewings. **At Your Service** is expert at helping those new to Paris to accomplish all the administrative tasks that can make your first months in a foreign country (particularly red-tape ridden France) fraught.

Learning *les arts de vivre*

Artist and portraitist **Karine de Rohan-Chabot**, holds workshops at **La Belle Ecole**, a school versed entirely in *les arts de vivre* (the art of living). Classes are in French or with English translation, with tutelage in cuisine, wine tasting, flower arranging, decorative arts, elegance and *savoir-vivre à la française*. It's rather like a modern-day finishing school. For an individual social or business etiquette advisor, trust the impeccably mannered Tamiko Zablith at **Minding Manners**.

Cooking workshops are available at both the **Ecole Le Cordon Bleu** and **Ecole Ritz Escoffier**; both also offer children's classes. Learn mixology with the inimitable Colin Peter Field, head barman of the **Hemingway Bar** at the Ritz, and anything from a Bloody Mary to a Mojito will be easily rustled up once home.

Oenophiles can find their way through the maze of French wine and discover some little known

10

delights from small producers at **Ô Chateau**'s excellent English-language tastings or at an evening arranged by the passionate wine-lover François Audouze for **Wine Dinners**. With a serious devotion to rare and old wines, François arranges exceptional dinners at a variety of Paris's best restaurants, which create a menu just for these extraordinary masterpieces of the winemaker's art.

To perfect your French, take a tip from the fashion industry: **Olivier Beaufour** is the man Paris's top modelling agencies call on to provide French lessons to their new talent. Models often have limited time for lessons, which has led Olivier to develop his own approach, giving students the skills to pick up the language easily over a short amount period. And if a sudden emergency calls you away, Olivier is more than happy to arrange your next lesson via video conference.

Floral fantasies

Floral creations reach a high art in a city where taking a bouquet is still de rigueur if you're invited out to dinner. **Odorantes** is a flower-delivery company that uniquely bases its superchic arrangements on scent, not colour, ensuring you have a room filled with heavenly natural aromas. **Les Mille-Feuilles**' creates unusual boutiques combining seasonal hues and original packaging. **Moulié Fleurs** is a Paris classic for grandiose bouquets as well as for floral decors for receptions, and many of its flowers are cultivated in its own nurseries in Brittany. For something less classic, order up something from Jacques Castagne at **Art et Végétal**, whose original creations may incorporate seeds and Plexiglas along with blooms, or **Marianne Robic** and **Pascal Mutel**, whose creations are beloved by many hotels and interior decorators.

Dress hire

Au Cor de Chasse is good to keep on hand for gentleman needing evening wear or special occasion attire, while **ABC Soirée** is on hand with that little black dress, evening gown or the hat, necklace and evening bag to finish off your party outfit.

Alice off course,
aliceoffcourse.com

10

Arriving in style

Executive Travel Services
© 01 45 54 98 60
chauffeur-limousine.com

HéliFrance
© 01 45 54 95 11
helifrance.com

Luxury & Services Rent a Car
42 av Montaigne, 8th
Ⓜ Franklin D. Roosevelt
© 01 72 74 10 48
luxury-rent-car.com
⊕ 5/F8

Tailor-made tours

4 roues sous 1 parapluie
© 01 42 96 04 91
4roues-sous-1parapluie.com

Edible Paris
edible-paris.com

Pamela H. Darling
© 01 45 67 62 81
eventsofprestige.com

Alice Off Course
© 06 83 26 86 20
aliceoffcourse.com

Hégé Service
© 06 60 09 86 53
hege-service.fr

Paris Muse
© 06 73 77 33 52
parismuse.com

Personal shopping

Atelier de Parfum Guerlain
68 av des Champs-Elysées, 8th
Ⓜ Franklin D. Roosevelt
© 01 45 62 11 21
guerlain.fr
⊕ 6/H7

Heather Price
© 08 71 04 55 45
priceparis.com

Paris Personal Shopper
parispersonalshopper.
susantabak.com

Eugénie de Rougé
(by appointment)
© 06 60 16 24 43
mademoisellelaparisienne.
blogspot.com

La Mode, Le Club
111 av Victor-Hugo, 16th
Ⓜ Victor Hugo
© 01 45 05 17 29
lamode-leclub.com
⊕ 5/A7

Vendôme Services
10 pl Vendôme, 1st
Ⓜ Opéra
© 01 53 45 66 83
vendome-services.com
⊕ 6/L8

Concierge services

At Your Service
℃ 01 47 95 12 90
atyourserviceparis.com

My Hôtel Particulier
℃ 06 81 86 75 02
myhotelparticulier.com

Ubiquicity
ubiquicity.com

Concierge Service
℃ 01 69 44 38 77
concierge-service.net

Quintessentially Paris
quintessentially.com

Wecandoo
℃ 06 71 25 10 75
wecandoo.net

Learning *les arts de vivre*

La Belle Ecole
7 r Scheffer, 16th
Ⓜ Rue de la Pompe
℃ 01 47 04 50 20
labelleecole.fr
⊕ 5/A9

Hemingway Bar
Hôtel Ritz, 15 pl
Vendôme, 1st
Ⓜ Opéra
℃ 01 43 16 30 50
ritz.com
⊕ 6/L8

Ô Château
℃ 01 44 73 97 80
o-chateau.com

Ecole Le Cordon Bleu
8 r Léon Delhomme, 15th
Ⓜ Vaugirard
℃ 01 53 68 22 50
cordonbleu.net
⊕ Off map

Karine de Rohan-Chabot
℃ 01 53 70 93 82
karinederohanchabot.com

Olivier Beaufour
14 r Ste-Croix de la
Bretonnerie, 4th
Ⓜ Hôtel de Ville
℃ 06 17 74 56 63
⊕ 11/R11

Ecole Ritz Escoffier
15 pl Vendôme, 1st
Ⓜ Opéra
℃ 01 43 16 30 50
ritz-paris.com
⊕ 6/L8

Minding Manners
91 r du Fbg St-Honoré, 8th
Ⓜ St Philippe du Roule
℃ 01 47 88 15 44
mindingmanners.com
⊕ 1-2/G5

Wine Dinners
℃ 06 07 81 48 25
wine-dinners.com

10

Floral fantasies

Art et Végétal J. Castagne
192 r de Tolbiac, 13th
Ⓜ Tolbiac
☎ 01 45 81 27 22
✛ Off map

Marianne Robic
39 r de Babylone, 7th
Ⓜ Sèvres Babylone
☎ 01 53 63 14 00
✛ 10/J13

Les Mille-Feuilles
2 r Rambuteau, 3rd
Ⓜ Rambuteau
☎ 01 42 78 32 93
les-mille-feuilles.com
✛ 11/R10

Moulié Fleurs
8 pl du Palais-Bourbon, 7th
Ⓜ Assemblée Nationale
☎ 01 45 51 78 43
mouliefleurs.com
✛ 10/I10

Odorantes
9 r Madame, 6th
Ⓜ St-Sulpice
☎ 01 42 84 03 00
✛ 10-14/M14

Pascal Mutel
6 carrefour de l'Odéon, 6th
Ⓜ Odéon
☎ 01 43 26 02 56
pascalmutel.com
✛ 11/N13

Dress hire

ABC Soirée
8 r Mignard, 16th
Ⓜ Rue de la Pompe
☎ 01 45 03 50 03
abcdsoiree.com
✛ Off map

Au Cor de Chasse
25 r de Condé, 6th
Ⓜ Odéon
☎ 01 43 26 51 89
aucorddechasse.fr
✛ 11/N13

10

See page 9 to scan the directory

INDEX

Page numbers in italics refer to chapter directories

11

11

11

11

4

19th

Laumière

Ourcq

Château
Rouge

Le
Chapelle

Stalingrad

Barbès-
Rochechouart

daurès

Bolivar

Anvers

St-
Georges

Gare
Du
Nord

Eurostar
Thalys

Louis
Blanc

Botzaris

Buttes
Chaumont

Poissonnière

Château-
Landon

Colonel
Fabien

Cadet

Gare
De
L'est

Jourdain

Le Pelletier

10th

8

Pyrénées

9th

Château
D'eau

Belleville

chelieu-
Drouot

Grands Boulevards

Goncourt

Bonne
Nouvelle

Strasbourg
Saint-
Denis

Jacques
Bonsergent

Couronnes

Bourse

Sentier

République

Temple

Ménilmontant

2th

Réaumur
Sébastopol

Arts-
et-
Métiers

Parmentier

St-
Maur

Oberkampf

Père
Lachaise

Étienne
Marcel

Filles
Du
Calvaire

St-
Ambroise

1st

Les
Halles

Rambuteau

3th

12

St-
Sébastien
Froissart

11th

Louvre-
Rivoli

Richard
Lenoir

Philippe-
Auguste

Pont-
Neuf

Châtelet

Hôtel
de
Ville

4th

Chemin-
Vert

Bréguet
Sabin

Voltaire

Cité

St-
Paul

Charonne

Saint-
Michel

Pont-
Marie

Bastille

Boulets-
Montreuil

abillon

Cluny-
la-
Sorbonne

Odéon

Ledru-
Rollin

Faidherbe-
Chaligny

Sully
Morland

Maubert-
Mutualité

16

Reuilly-
Diderot

5

Cardinal
Lemoine

Quai
De La
Rapée

Gare
de
Lyon

5th

Jussieu

Montgallet

Luxembourg

Place
Monge

12th

Gare
D'austerlitz

Bercy

Dugommier

Port Royal

Censier
Daubenton

St-marcel

Map

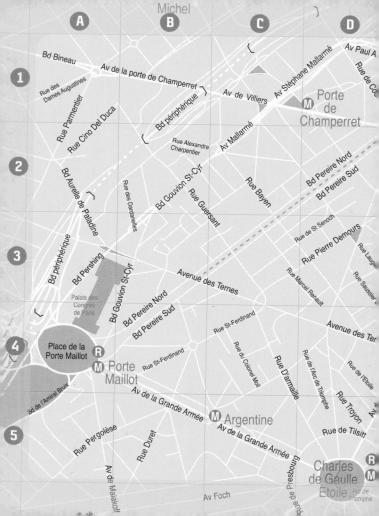

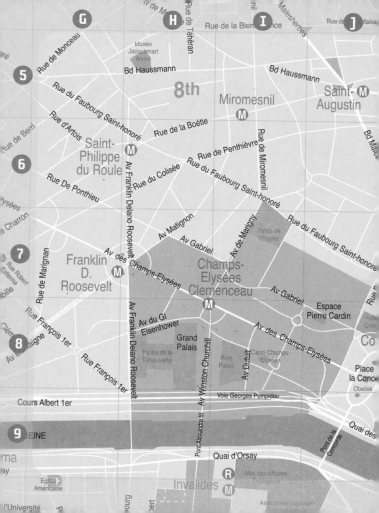

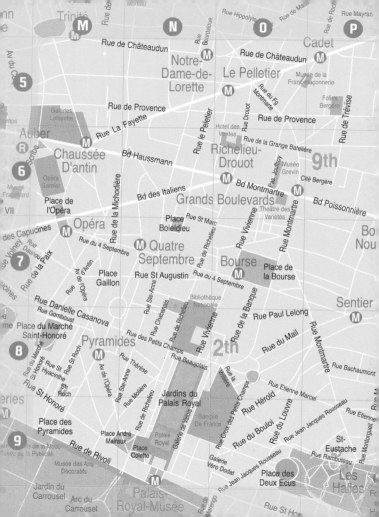

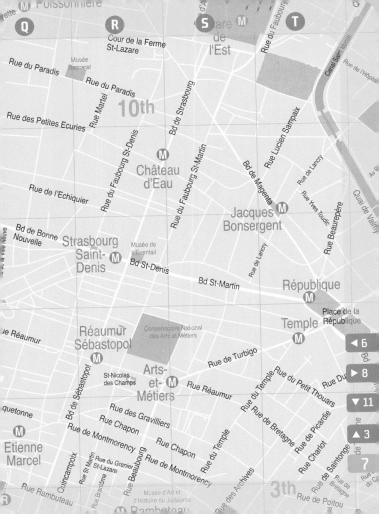

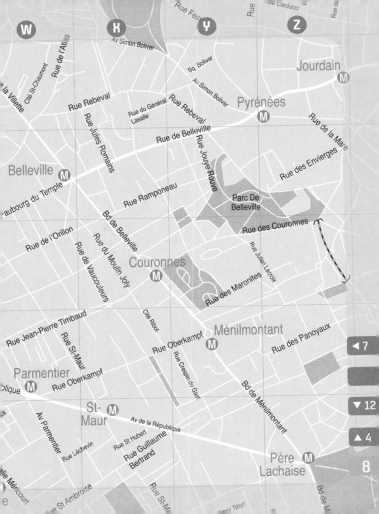

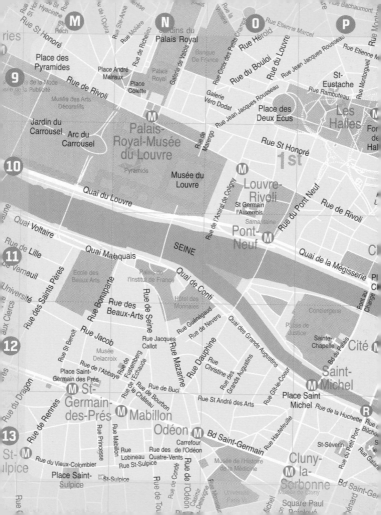

Av du Gén... du Pi...

A　　　**B**　　　**C**　　**D**

Jiffren

Rue de la Fédéra

Rue St-Saëns

M Bir Hakeim

Bd de Grenelle

Rue Marguerite Yourcenar

13

Av du Président
R Kennedy

Michel Ple
Radio-France

Proprio

Quai de Grenelle

Rue du Docteur Finlay

Dupleix

M Bd de Grenelle

14

Rue Robert de Flers

Rue St Charles

Rue Béatrix Dussane

Rue Tiphaine

Rue Letellier

Rue de l'Ingénieur Robert Keller

Rue Beaugrenelle

Rue Ginoux

Rue Georges Citerne

Rue de Lourmel

Rue du Théatre

Av. **M** Emile Zola

Rue du T

15

Charles Michels **M**

Av Emile Zola

Rue Violet

Rue du T

Rue des Quatre Frères Peignot

16

Rue St Charles

Rue Ste-Lucie

Rue de Lourmel

Rue de la Rosière

M Commerc

Rue Lakanal

Rue de la Convention

Rue de Javel

Rue des Entrepreneurs

Rue Lacordaire

Félix Faure

M

imetière Grenelle

17

Rue de Lourmel

Boucicaut

M

Rue des Frères Morane

Rue de la Croix Nivert

Rue de l'Abbé Groult

Av Félix Faure

Rue Henri Bocquillon

Rue de la Convention

Rue Lecou

M **Lourmel**

PARIS MET

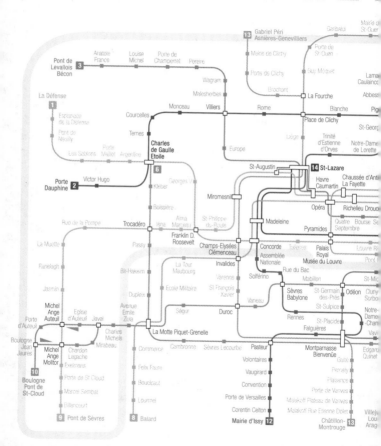

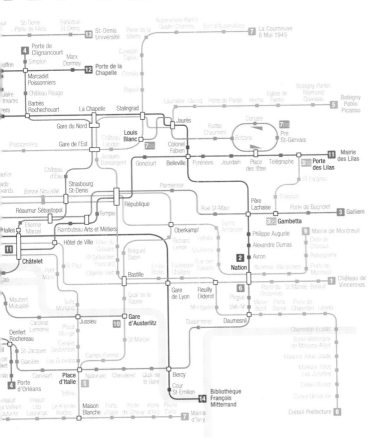

ROPOLITAN

OTHER TITLES IN THE AUTHENTIK COLLECTION

Europe
Gourmet Paris
Artistik Paris

Chic London
Gourmet London
Artistik London

FORTHCOMING AUTHENTIK GUIDES – SPRING 2008

North America
Gourmet New York
Chic New York
Artistik New York

Europe
Barcelona
Berlin
Milan
Prague

Asia
Beijing
Bali

Africa
Marrakech
Cape Town

FORTHCOMING WINE ROADBOOKS – AUTUMN 2008

France
Bordeaux
Burgundy
Champagne
Loire Valley

Italy
Tuscany

Spain
Rioja

North America
Napa Valley
Sonoma County

Visit www.authentikbooks.com
to find out more about AUTHENTIK titles

K

Alison Culliford

Alison Culliford started her career at Condé-Nast in London and worked on several national papers before taking flight as a roving travel writer for British Airways High Life, covering destinations including China, Labrador and the Republic of Georgia. In 2001 she touched down in Paris and realised she never wanted to leave. While working for Time Out Paris she took a diploma in haute couture, learning the secrets of petites mains. She is the author of three books : Paris Revisited (Chrysalis Books), Night + Day Paris (Pulse Guides) and France: Instructions for Use (Illustrata Press), and lives amid the shabby grandeur of the Faubourg St-Denis.

Alain Bouldouyre

Gentleman artist Alain Bouldouyre captures in his fine line drawings what our *Chic Paris* author conjures up in words – the quintessence of the city. Art director for *Senso* magazine, and author/illustrator of numerous travel books, Alain fast tracks around the world in hand-stitched loafers, a paintbox and sketch pad his most precious accessories.

COMMERCIAL LICENSING

Authentik illustrations, text and listings are available for commercial licensing at www.authentikartwork.com

ORIGINAL ARTWORK

All signed and numbered original illustrations by Alain Bouldouyre published in this book are available for sale. Original artwork by Alain Bouldouyre is delivered framed with a certificate of authenticity.

CUSTOM-MADE EDITIONS

Authentik books make perfect, exclusive gifts for personal or corporate purposes.

Special editions, including personalized covers, excerpts from existing titles and corporate imprints, can be custom produced.

All enquiries should be addressed to Wilfried LeCarpentier at wl@authentikbooks.com